Globejotting

How to Write Extraordinary Travel Journals

(and still have time to enjoy your trip!)

Dave Fox

Portland • Oregon

Cover and interior design: Masha Shubin
Editor: Linda Weinerman

Cover illustrations: building elements from Corel Gallery © 2003, london skyline © 2008 Leon Bonaventura (iStockPhoto.com), open book © 2008 Stephen Dumayne (iStockPhoto.com)
Interior illustrations by Masha Shubin

A similar version of the essay, "Saunas: The Naked Truth," appears in the book *Rite of Passage: Tales of Backpacking 'Round Europe,* © 2003 Lonely Planet.

Paperback
ISBN-13 978-1-59299-344-4 | ISBN-10 1-59299-344-3

Kindle
ISBN-13 978-1-59299-557-8 | ISBN-10 1-59299-557-8

Publisher: Inkwater Press | www.inkwaterpress.com

Printed in the U.S.A.
All paper is acid free and meets all ANSI standards for archival quality paper.

5 7 9 10 8 6 4

Contents

Acknowledgments

Welcome to the acknowledgments! This is the part of a book that most people don't actually read, unless they hope they will be acknowledged. My duty here is to acknowledge every person who has in some way helped or inspired the production of this book.

That list, however, includes hundreds of friends and strangers around the world who, over the years, have offered me couches to crash on, sandwiches to munch on, or stories to feed my soul during moments when my solo travels would have otherwise felt lonely. It includes throngs of friends at home who think I'm kind of weird, but hang out with me anyway. It includes all the flight attendants and airline ticket agents who get verbally harangued by crazy people, yet still show up for work so the rest of us can fly. It includes people on my tours, students in my classes, and visitors to my websites who e-mail me with feedback or stories of their own. It even includes all of the clerks at my local grocery store, without whom I would have starved to death long ago because my subsistence farming skills are severely lacking.

Acknowledging all of you would be difficult. There just isn't room. Furthermore, every time I type up the acknowledgments section for a new book, I tremble with fear that I might omit someone very important in a moment of looming deadline pressure. So before we go any further, let's just do this:

Thank you. Yes, you. For whatever reason you have picked up this book, you rock. And you deserve to be mentioned by name, so here...go grab a pen or pencil and enter your name below:

I, Dave Fox, would like to thank

____

for his/her never-ending awesomeness.

Okay, now that I've covered all of my bases, allow me to mention a few specific people who might be too busy or shy to fill in the above blank.

Thanks to my parents. Had they forgotten to give birth to me, writing this book would have been very difficult. But that's not all they did. They also had the courage to take me to confusing foreign places when I was young and whiny. Now that I am old and whiny, I go to such places all by myself, but it was helpful having them along in the beginning, when I was too small to carry my own suitcase.

Thanks to the entire staff at Inkwater Press. Nobody there is responsible for my birth, but they have all helped bring this book into the world. Thanks especially to Jeremy Solomon for approaching me about the idea, and for buying me tasty Vietnamese food when I came to Portland; to my editor, Linda Weinerman, for her epic knowledge of obscure punctuation rules; to Masha Shubin, whose graphic design prowess is always served with a side-order of witty banter; and to Jo Ristow and

Lauren Rizzo, for helping fling my travel journaling gospel out to the masses.

Jeni Enns and Darbi Macy offered invaluable feedback on my manuscript, and worded their constructive criticism in ways that were always honest, yet never soul-crushing. Cynthia Orr's tips on motivation were a huge motivation for me in writing my chapter about motivation. Michaelanne Jerome gave me a refresher course on French reflexive verbs – a topic that occupies a mere half-sentence in this book, but she helped me get it right.

Thanks to Rick Steves, who has kept me traveling all these years, and to Brad Cilley for helping launch my own travel journaling tour endeavors.

And finally, gargantuan thanks to Kattina Rabdau for her unflinching patience with my crazy travel schedule, for encouraging me to keep writing even when my writing-induced neurosis gets annoying, and for always keeping life a fun adventure.

CHAPTER 1

The Ultimate Souvenir

You're going on a big trip? Woohoo! The rest of us are very jealous.

What are you going to bring? Some clean underwear, we hope. A toothbrush and one of those travel-sized toothpaste tubes so the cool people you meet won't run away. A passport, perhaps, if you're leaving the country. And what about a camera? Sure. Everyone brings a camera on vacation, so they can return home with fascinating snapshots of their left index finger – in what is probably an exotic locale, only we're not sure because we can't see the locale behind the finger.

How about a travel journal of some sort? An 89-cent spiral notebook? Or maybe some schmancy leather-bound volume in which to document your journey? Since you are reading this book, I will now invoke my extremely impressive psychic powers and predict that yes, a travel journal of some sort is on your packing list.

Excellent! So what are you going to do with this amazing travel journal? Are you going to write in it every day and use it as a record of your wanderings that will remain accurate even when your brain is old and fuzzy someday?* Or are you going to do what most people do with their travel journals: jot down a few sentences on days one and two, then leave it until day six when you decide you can no longer recall what happened on days three, four, and five, therefore the most effective use of your journal for the duration of your journey will be to serve as ballast at the bottom of your bag?

* Hey, no offense. Our brains are all getting older and fuzzier, one day at a time.

Seriously, that is what happens to thousands of travel journals every year. The owners of these journals return home safe and sound, but the journals themselves die a quiet and lonely death.

Oh, the humanity.

Then there's another breed of travel journaler who *does* manage to write on most days. Yay for them, but there's still a problem: Many of these every-day journalers dislike what they write because their journals sound so...everyday. Their writing is like grocery lists – pedestrian, step-by-step accounts of their trips, bundles of words that ooze with clichés and feigned excitement.

"My trips are always so exciting," a woman confessed one time during a class I was teaching, "but my journals are always boring. What's wrong with me?"

"Wrong with you?" I said. "Nothing is wrong with you. You are totally normal. It's the successful travel journalers, the ones who come home with books full of enthralling, emotion-packed, detail-saturated stories, who are the abnormal ones. Sadly, the norm is that most people's travel journaling endeavors flop, just like yours have."

Hi! Welcome to my book. My goal for the next 175 pages is to help you break free from these totally normal journaling syndromes. I want to help you become one of the abnormal ones, one of the successful journalers. I want you to become a travel journaling superhero. Maybe someday you'll even get your own action figure.

But let's not get ahead of ourselves. I've got a few things to teach you before you can go shopping for a cape.

And hey...maybe you already do write super-amazing travel journals. Maybe you're a travel journaling rock star. That's awesome, dude! Seriously, if you already are a travel journaling rock star, I am now waving a cigarette lighter in the air in homage to your awesomeness. But stick around anyway. I've got cool new techniques to make your journals even rock-starrier.

Photographic Memories

I was working as a guest lecturer on a cruise ship in the South Pacific recently. As we sped toward Samoa, I took the stage in the ship's auditorium and opened my travel journaling talk with the same question I always start my talks with: "How many of you aren't wearing any underwear today?"

Just kidding. That's not really how I usually start my talks.

What I really start my talks with is, "How many of you bring a camera when you travel?"

As I asked this question, nearly every person in the room shot their hand up, as if to say, "Duh! Of course we bring our cameras on vacation, dummy!"

I followed with another question: "And how many of you keep a journal when you travel?"

With this second question, the response wasn't so confident. About a third of the people in the room raised their hands. Among those who did, most did so timidly. Many had uneasy winces, as if I had just asked them to confess something embarrassing and dirty. Others were hiding behind the person in front of them.

"So you all use cameras to remember your travels, but when

I brought up journaling, a lot of you started to look seasick." I said. "What's going on?"

A polite yet awkward silence hung in the air for a moment. People don't want to be rude and tell the journaling guy they like photography better. But eventually, a man in the third row got bold. "Journaling takes too long."

He was right – sort of. Photography is quicker and easier than writing things down. It only takes a few seconds to aim, frame, and shoot. We can zap a moment and get on with our day. We don't have to worry later about recalling what we've seen. We don't have to carve precious time out of our too-short vacation. Once a photograph is taken, the memory is captured.

Journaling is more time consuming. But quick, easy, and accurate as photography is, taking pictures has its limits. Photos capture slivers of time – fractions of seconds confined within the walls of our viewfinders. A well-written travel journal can record all sorts of things you just can't capture with a camera.

Photography is a visual art. Its primary focus is what we see. In writing, we can document *all* the senses – not just sights, but sounds, tastes, smells, and physical sensations. We meet a lot of people when we travel – interesting people, beautiful people, weird people, ugly people, helpful people, grouchy people, smelly people, tasty people, all kinds of people who become unwitting characters in our own personal travel tales – and for all kinds of reasons, we can't always photograph them. Even when we can, we still miss out on so much about them – the way they spoke, the way they moved, the way they laughed, blinked, ate, sneezed, walked, smelled, sneered, begged, cowered, or kissed. Photographs can't capture the stories they told us, the wisdom they imparted, the ways they helped us, taught us, inspired us, or freaked us out. And the shortcomings of photography extend beyond people. Often, places don't photograph well either. Rainy weather dulls the lighting. An angry museum docent is practicing his two words of English: "No photo! No photo!" We're in motion so our subject is blurred. Or maybe the landscape's just too vast to squeeze it all into a photograph. In a journal, we can overcome all of those issues.

There's something even bigger we can't capture on film. I call it our "inner journey." Your inner journey is everything that goes on inside your brain when you travel – the unique thoughts, emotions, and reactions you experience in unfamiliar surroundings. This inner journey is often the most powerful part of a trip. Venturing into unfamiliar places can spark big revelations about ourselves. All too often, however, once we return home, these discoveries are lost, buried beneath our everyday mind clutter. We can't photograph any of the things that flit through our minds as we expose ourselves to unfamiliar places, but we can write about them – and return to our pages long after our trips are finished for refresher courses on the stuff we've learned while traveling.

This having been said, I don't want an angry mob of photo aficionados on my doorstep, threatening me with sharp gardening tools or big zoom lenses, so allow me to stress that I am not anti-photography. Not at all! I love taking pictures when I travel. Later, I'll even teach you ways to merge your photos and journals together. So by all means, take lots of pictures when you travel. But write too. Your journals will help you remember aspects of a trip that photos alone can't capture. And your left index finger is less likely to get in the way of a journal.

How to Use This Book

Rule number one: Break the rules.

There are lots of different ways you can use this book. My number one goal is that you have fun with it.

I'm going to approach travel journaling from several different angles – journaling to remember your trips, journaling to share your experiences with friends and family, journaling for personal growth, and journaling as a step toward getting published, to name a few. Different people have different writing goals, and some of these chapters might resonate with your own personal interests more than others. So if you come across parts of this book that don't click with your journaling goals, move along to the parts that do. You won't hurt my feelings.

I'll also offer suggestions for successful ways to approach your journaling – approaches that have been successful for me, and/or students in my seminars – but this isn't a high school English class, and I don't want to be a stodgy, set-in-his-ways teacher. I'm not going to flunk you if you do things differently from the ways I suggest. So find what works best for you. I will even let you chew gum. In return, I humbly request that you not scrawl nasty things about me on bathroom walls, okay?

In the coming pages, I'll teach you how to break free from conventional journaling styles, and write in bold new ways. You'll discover how to be more aware of your surroundings as you go about your day, absorbing more details and then writing those details into your pages. In doing so, you will not only write better, you'll travel better too, getting more deeply in tune with the places you wander through.

You can learn every brilliant writing technique in the world, however, and if you can't find the time and fearlessness to use them, these techniques are useless. So we'll also tackle the time and fearlessness issues. I will teach you how to write faster – and better – than you ever have.

Journaling should not be an interruption in your travels. It should not suck precious time out of your vacations. Vacations are supposed to be fun, and if journaling isn't fun, you're not going to want to do it. So we'll look at ways to integrate journaling into your journeys without sacrificing travel experiences. If you're cooped up in your hotel room with your nose in your notebook while an exciting world is happening outside, you're not journaling constructively. We'll look at alternative ways, times, and places to write. Travel journaling shouldn't feel like an irritating homework assignment that you must do when you really want to go out and play. You *should* go out and play – as much as possible.

And fearlessness? What do I mean by that? Writing can feel scary sometimes. Especially writing about ourselves. There are lots of psychological forces that can drag down our writing. Every great writer experiences self-doubt about his or her words at times. With journaling, we have the added challenge of writing about our own, occasionally spooky emotions. Putting feelings on paper can make them seem more tangible, and sometimes we're timid about getting so close to our thoughts. We'll talk about that. I'll teach you how to write bravely.

So in this book, you will learn how to write faster, better, more constructively, and more fearlessly than so-called "normal" journalers write. And you – you journaling-superhero-in-training, you – are going to learn these things by writing along with me.

In most of these chapters, you'll have an opportunity or two to hop in the "Flight Simulator" and take the lessons you are learning for a test flight. You wouldn't try to fly a plane before getting some practice on the ground, would you? We're going to take the same approach with journaling, so that once you're really traveling, you won't crash your journals. The more you write at home before you go off on your next odyssey, the easier your writing will flow once you're in a real travel journaling environment. Think of it this way: You can buy an electric guitar and let it gather dust, but don't pick it up five years later and expect to magically sound like Jimi Hendrix. The same holds true for writing: The more you practice, the faster you'll become Super Travel Journaling Person.

So I suggest you buy yourself a notebook of some sort to do

the "Flight Simulator" exercises in. Or if you're wrapped up in the digital age, create a file on your computer and type them. If, however, you don't have time for that – perhaps you are hastily scanning these pages, already en route to your next destination – that's fine. If you don't have time to practice before you go, you can still learn these techniques just by reading this book. Skim quickly if you must, and jump to the sections that seem most helpful to you. Read through the exercises even if you don't have time to do them. As you travel, they'll serve as prompts for your writing.

I'm also going to share some of my own travel journals with you. I hope you feel at least a little special about this because I had a big fight with my editors over this. You know how you're shy about sharing your private diaries with others? So am I.

For reasons I'll explain in a little while, I believe your primary travel journals are things you should write for yourself, and yourself alone. You shouldn't censor your thoughts for fear that someone else might read what you've written.* And if you've promised yourself not to share your words with others, you must keep that promise.

*We'll talk later about when and how to share your journals with others.

I've made a similar promise to myself. But such a promise gets messy when you suddenly find yourself with editors offering you a book deal, and simultaneously demanding that you expose your travel journals to the world.

So we have reached a compromise, my editors and I. All of the sample journal entries in this book are blurbs I have deemed suitable for public consumption. A few of them I have rewritten – either because the original version was too personal, or because the original version was too lame. Yes, lame. My travel journals, back before I had aspirations of becoming Super Travel Journaling Man, were, at times, incredibly lame. I've gotten better over time because I've journaled a lot. So I have polished up some of these earlier bursts of journaling because the purpose of including them here is to show you good journaling, not lameness. Between each chapter, you will find a hopefully-not-lame, quick journal entry from my travels. If you like them, you can read lots more of my journal entries and travel tales, share your success stories, offer me feedback on how this book's working out for you, sign up for online classes, learn about my in-person classes and international journaling tours, and check out other cool travel journaling stuff on my website at **traveljournaling.com**.

How Travel Journaling Changed My Life

I was born and raised in the United States, but shortly before my eighth birthday, my family moved to England for a year. My parents understood our year abroad would be a unique experience that would stand out above the other years in our lives, so whenever there was a school holiday, we'd travel.

Some of our adventures were road trips in the fluorescent orange station wagon that came with the house we were renting – to the battlefields of Hastings or the Roman ruins in Bath. Other journeys were farther flung. We wrinkled our noses at Dutch fish markets and had summer snowball fights in the Swiss Alps. We splashed among Greek island jellyfish and rode camels in northern Africa.

When we first arrived in England, my parents gave me a big red book. It was a hardback book – intended to be a day-to-day calendar for adults with busy schedules. I used the book differently. Whenever we traveled outside our South London neighborhood, I would write mini essays recapping where we had been. Even at age eight, I got it that I was having a different kind of year from the rest of my life so far. I wanted to remember where I'd been, so I wrote about our adventures. I've been journaling ever since.

More than a decade later, in college, I went through the post-adolescent meltdown commonly known as "sophomore slump." I began to wonder what I was doing with my life. I had lived a childhood year in England, and a teenage year as a foreign exchange student in Norway. I didn't feel totally American anymore. I didn't feel European either. I just felt kind of lost, like I was missing something, like there was a big, big world out there, beyond the confines of my cinderblock dorm room, and I needed to go see it. So I took time off from school, saved money to travel, and spent three months on a super-low-budget romp through Europe, sleeping in youth hostels, on trains, on beaches, and on train station floors.*

*This was an amazing trip in a variety of ways, but the coolest part was that it totally freaked out my parents.

I had a goal for that journey. I wanted to write a book – a memoir of the places I visited and the people I met. So along the way, I journaled obsessively, sometimes for a couple of hours each day. I didn't want to miss a single detail.

Don't panic. I'm not going to tell you to journal for several hours a day in your own travels. On the contrary, I had not yet learned the time-saving techniques presented in the next chapter.

After I returned home, I spent two years polishing my journals into a travel memoir. When I was finished, I realized I had broken a completely useless world record. I had just written a 550-page manuscript – the longest version in history of "What I Did on My Summer Vacation." I was still a fledgling writer. My skills had not yet evolved to the level of professional author. That book, in that form, would never be published. I buried my manuscript at the bottom of a desk drawer, all but forgetting about it, until several years later.

Then in my mid-20s, I approached travel writer and television host Rick Steves to grovel for a job. Rick asked if I'd be willing to share some of my writing, so I sent him a few of the chapters that had evolved from my journals. He hired me, based on those chapters, and for more than a decade, I've worked for him as a tour guide, living my dream of a career in international travel.*

*My other dream career is to be a superhero, but nobody seems to be hiring these days.

Eventually, I did publish my first book. *Getting Lost: Mishaps of an Accidental Nomad* became my collection of humorous stories about things that have gone wrong in my lifetime of overseas wanderings – starting with my childhood in England, spanning forward to my adult years, guiding tours and working in the travel industry. I dusted off the pages of my earlier book attempt and rewrote some of them. The book I wrote in college, once condemned to the bottom of my desk drawer for eternity, eventually made it to life in published form.

My first book, my international career, my adult life as a professional traveler, all happened because of my travel journals. So did that South Pacific speaking gig that I mentioned with irritating nonchalance a couple of pages ago. What began as a hobby has brought me work on six continents.*

*And if anyone on Antarctica wants to fly me in for a seminar on continent number seven, I'll do it for a discount.

I can't promise you becoming a dedicated travel journaler will land you book deals or globetrotting careers, but I will promise you this: Follow the techniques in this book, and over time, you'll notice your travel experiences growing richer. You'll gain a deeper understanding of who you are and how you interact with the world around you. And you will learn to capture your travels in ways that keep your memories burning bright for years to come.

Ready for Take-Off!

What do you think of when you think of a souvenir? A T-shirt? A piece of artwork? A splurgy bottle of wine? A snow globe or a floaty pen? When some people travel, they bring along an empty suitcase to fill with purchases along the way. Others travel light, savoring their memories instead. Whatever your own personal travel style is, when most of us think of the word, "souvenir," we think of material possessions – elegant or kitschy – that we purchase on a journey.

But the word "souvenir" has a deeper meaning. It's a word we've swiped from the French language. In French, *se souvenir* is the verb for "to remember." A souvenir is a memory. In English, it has come to mean something we accumulate when we are away from home that will help us remember a place we've visited.

For years, when I thought of "souvenirs," one of the first things that came to mind was the T-shirt vendors who hang out outside the Colosseum in Rome. For five euros (or the equivalent in US dollars or Japanese yen), they'll sell you a T-shirt with a sketch by Michelangelo or a cartoon of some ancient ruins. Tourists go crazy over these cheap T-shirts. I've watched people flock around the streetside vendors and walk away with armloads of them. And, I will confess, I've bought a couple myself.

When I return home to Seattle after a season of tour guiding, one of the first things I do is sort my laundry into two piles: clothes I need to wash, and clothes I need to burn. After living out of a backpack for a couple of months, some clothing takes on a whole new aroma, and it's not pretty. But if I've bought one of these cheap souvenir T-shirts, it goes in the wash pile.

I put it in my washing machine. Then I put it in my dryer. An hour later, when I take it out of the dryer, my "souvenir" has shrunk so much, it won't even fit my cat.

And we call this a memory?

Traveling is one of the most adventurous, eye-opening things we can do with our lives. A two-week journey reverberates much longer than the two weeks we're away. For months, even years ahead of time, we're filled with anticipation as we make plans and wonder what our trip will be like. Once we return home, we may be far from the places we have visited, but the memories linger. Many journeys, once we have taken them, are experiences we carry with us for the rest of our lives.

Like T-shirts, however, memories fade over time. They become contorted. Details become fuzzy. Names or faces of people we met are things we can no longer recall. Sights, sounds, and smells become dulled. And saddest of all, sometimes the powerful revelations we experience, away from our usual lives, fade into our mental ether as we recoil back to our default personality, the one that has been shaped by our familiar culture. When this happens, potential opportunities for personal growth are lost.

Travel journals don't shrink. They endure. If you journal about your experiences as you travel, you'll collect your memories for easy retrieval whenever you want.

If you have tried travel journaling before and felt unsatisfied with the results, or if you have never journaled before and want to begin, this book will help you grow as both a traveler and a writer. So, friends, unfasten your seatbelts and follow me. Prepare to travel like you have never traveled before – and to return home with the ultimate souvenir – your own memories, true stories kept alive and vivid in the words you scribble as you wander our planet.

Dave's Diaries

Suva, Fiji

Our first steps into an unfamiliar place can jar us emotionally like a plunge into an icy lake shocks us physically. We don't know where we're going. We're surrounded by unfamiliar sights, smells, and sounds. We might feel vulnerable, or fatigued from the journey, or frustrated by a language barrier. These things all glob together into what is commonly called "culture shock." This journal entry is about a culture shock experience I had – one I wasn't expecting.

Usually when I travel to foreign places, I'm braced for that initial jolt of confusion, not to mention the con artists and other unscrupulous creatures who sometimes prey upon confused and vulnerable tourists. I'm usually ready for these moments, but in Fiji, I let my guard down.

I was working on a cruise ship in a part of the world I had never been. My friend Lisa, an experienced international traveler herself, was on board with me. Our image of Fiji, prior to arrival, had been the image many Americans have – a faraway, warm and idyllic place, calming and peaceful (as long as they're not having a military coup). My first hour on land was not what I expected. It intimidated me to the point that I almost fled. But I stayed, and rekindled an important lesson I had learned years earlier: First impressions of faraway places can be deceiving. We must be patient with a new destination when it greets us with an initial shock.

Journaling about my uneasy arrival on Fiji, and my major shift in attitude over the course of a few hours, captured my full experience – good and bad. More importantly, writing honestly about my own fears and judgments reminded me not to flee from future destinations when my first few moments aren't what I've anticipated.

Soggy Tubas in Suva

Buy a space heater and put it in your bathroom. Crank

it up to high. Turn on the shower, full blast, at its hottest temperature. No fan allowed. Wait 20 minutes for it to get good and humid.

There. You have just simulated Fiji's November climate in your own home.

Oh, and by the way, Fiji is a conservative culture. According to my guidebook, long pants are recommended when you're not at the beach.

Fiji has a reputation for being a tropical paradise, but the palm tree beaches in the tour brochures don't exist in Suva, the country's capital. They are elsewhere on the island.

Suva is a chaotic place with a third-worldly feel. At first glance, it's intimidating. It's got a hard exterior. You have to struggle if you want to get below the surface to its sweeter parts.

We docked at eight this morning. Lisa and I argued over who would shower first. We both wanted 10 more minutes of sleep. The crew bar the night before – a bar below sea level in the lower recesses of the ship that's off limits to regular passengers – had been a lively scene – not the kind of place you should linger too long if you have sightseeing plans in the morning.

We were on land by 10. The second we left the shipyard, we were surrounded by friendly Fijians. But it wasn't the kind of friendly I had encountered in New Caledonia two days earlier. It was the kind of friendly I had feared in New Caledonia and never discovered – the "special price for you, my friend" kind of friendly. My guidebook described typical scams on the island, and our new-found "friends" were in the first steps of exactly what the book was describing.

We ran the gauntlet of con artists, made our way to the center of town, and tried to locate an ATM. We found one, with at least 20 people waiting. We took our place in line.

"*Bula*," a man said to me – Fijian for hello. "Are you wanting to take out money?"

Suspicious, I answered in Norwegian. "*Jeg snakker ikke engelsk*." I don't speak English.

He persisted. "You can't use this machine here. It's only for local bank cards. If you want to use a Visa card, you must go around the corner."

He was telling the truth. He was the first person to approach us who really wanted to help. I felt irritated with myself that I'd felt a need to keep my guard up. I suddenly learned English and thanked him.

But the next two machines we tried would not give us money, and our American cash was back on the ship. We had to go retrieve it.

Once again, we made our way past the Suva welcoming committee. I didn't want to deal with any of this.

I needed to reframe my thinking.

I've encountered aggressive selling and/or brazen scamming many times in my travels. It's sad that it happens because it gives visitors an unfair impression of a place. Take the Grand Bazaar in Istanbul, for example. I used to feel intimidated there. Now I understand Turkey well enough to love the chaos. But Fiji was too distant from the cultures I am familiar with. In new surroundings, the hassles felt so much more intimidating.

Back at the ship, Lisa and I both confessed we didn't want to leave. Sitting by the pool all day would be so much easier. But we were in Fiji, damn it. Fiji! We needed to give it another chance.

Suva, Take 2: I left my little backpack on the ship this time. Not having it dangling from my shoulder, I felt like less of a target. Now anything worth stealing – my wallet or my camera – was in my pocket. Pickpockets don't worry me anymore. I know their games.

When we reached the center of Suva, we started to relax. Away from the docks, people were the sincere kind of friendly. Some streets felt more like India-Lite than the South Pacific. Fiji has a sizable Indian population – descendants of indentured servants brought to the islands long ago. We ate lunch at a vegetarian Hare Krishna restaurant. It came recommended by an American friend of Lisa who used to live in Suva. Four Fijian dollars – about $2.50 US – was enough for a feast. We struggled to fit the food inside of us. It became downright painful, but in a poor part of the world, American visitors leaving food just wouldn't be cool.

Shop owners and taxi drivers had no qualms about telling us all Americans are very rich. We tried to explain that isn't true. American visitors to Fiji might be rich. (Or they might be cruise ship employees.) It was hard explaining we have poverty in America too – and it felt unnecessarily defensive.

On our way to the museum, we stumbled across a volleyball tournament. We chatted with spectators, and watched until we couldn't take the heat anymore. Then we continued, through a garden of tropical fauna, to a building housing centuries-old outrigger canoes and cannibal forks. Cannibalism existed here as recently as the 19th century.

In the mid-afternoon, we stumbled upon a local market. We thought we'd stick our heads in for a quick peek, but we ended up lingering. Vendors sold taro root and some of the strangest fruits I've ever seen. Young children played in their parents' stalls. One girl of about two was running around with an eight-inch butcher's knife.

Walking back to the ship, random people would smile and say, "*Bula*." This was the friendliness I'd seen in Nouméa two days earlier. It was real. It's how most Fijians live.

As we waited to sail onward toward the equator, a perfectly timed thunderstorm began. Seattle rarely has thunderstorms and I miss them. The skies opened up.

A party was just getting started on a covered deck. Down below, on land, a Fijian marching band was playing for us, and dock workers were dancing in the rain. Between songs, the tuba players would turn their instruments upside down to empty out the water. I had to admire people who would stand in the middle of a pounding downpour to play music.

I need to remember this day in my future travels. First impressions of unfamiliar places are often negative. Give yourself time to get beneath the prickly surface and you'll be rewarded.

CHAPTER 2

Speed Journaling

Keeping Up with Your Journey

Traveling and journaling must be approached with opposite philosophies: Travel too quickly and you miss out on things. Journal too slowly and...you miss out on things.

I learned this lesson on my first visit to Istanbul, Turkey, in the summer of 1989. My first few hours, fresh off the bus from the tamer port town of Kuşadası, all I wanted was to be airlifted back to the mundane familiarity of someplace more Western. I had just dog-paddled into the deep end of the culture shock pool. I felt in over my head.

Overbearing shoe shiners and carpet sellers whacked me with sales pitches. Traffic jammed the streets like water in a high-pressure fire hose. Crossing the street felt as dangerous as trying to sip from that hose. Five times a day, calls to prayer spilled from minarets throughout the city – a sound my American mind had subconsciously learned, from too many TV news reports, to equate with something spooky and unsafe. My first day in Turkey's most populous city, my attitudes had been colored by fearful, condescending stereotypes. I wanted to run away, but I didn't. I knew if I left, I'd never muster the courage to return.

So I hung on, and within a few days, I realized what a paranoid freak I had been when I first arrived. The only people who were seriously out to get me were the ones in my head. Out in the real world, most Turks were delightful. Even the carpet sellers turned out to be fun-loving conversationalists once I opened up my wallet and showed them I didn't have enough cash to buy anything.

As my perspective shifted, I extended my stay, cutting out other planned stops in Eastern Europe for just another day or two, or seven, or twelve, in my new favorite spot on the planet. After 17 days, the once-intimidating chaos of this sprawling, Middle Eastern metropolis felt mesmerizing.

I did the obligatory sightseeing, visiting Topkapı Palace, the Blue Mosque, Ağa Sofia Cathedral, and the cistern that reflected multi-colored lights into cool darkness. But I got my sightseeing over with quickly so I could get on with what I really wanted to do. My favorite thing was to walk – no plan, no map – into the back streets.

Kids with soccer balls would swarm around and invite me into their games. Adults would stare, more shyly than the children, probably wondering what I was doing away from my tribe of tourists. Neighborhood teahouses offered front-row seats at backgammon throw-downs, where the local spectators were as passionate about their evening entertainment as American sports junkies are about Monday Night Football. I grew to savor the beauty in the muezzins' voices as they called people to prayer. I even learned how to cross the street.

Istanbul still overwhelmed me, but in a good way. I found ways to manage the intensity. I'd spend my days wandering, gobbling down newly discovered delicacies, flooding my eyes, my ears, my nose, my mind, with stimulus after stimulus. By late afternoon, overloaded with new impressions, I would retreat to the youth hostel courtyard, a calm oasis where other travelers sat, shared stories and beers, and decompressed from their days. The courtyard was a perfect place to write.

One afternoon, I found myself with my nose in my journal, my face wadded into an overthinking ball of concentration as I struggled to recall every detail of the past several days. I had fallen behind. After an hour of writing, I was nowhere near caught up. I began to resent my journal. No matter how much time I spent, it seemed I would never get back on track.

"You look really intense," said Anna, a Swede I had met at the hostel a few days earlier.

"There's too much to write," I whined. "This is impossible."

Anna looked at me like I was crazy – which I partially was. "How many pages have you written today?" she asked.

"Six."

"And you're how many days behind?"

"Four."

"You're writing too much," she said. "And look at your handwriting."

I looked at my handwriting. "What's wrong with it?"

"Nothing," Anna said. "That's the problem. Are you trying to write a travel diary or win a handwriting contest?"

Anna wasn't a writer, and as far as I know, she wasn't keeping a journal either, but she had a skill I lacked. She understood that the way to get things done is to *do* them. Not do them perfectly. Just do them.

As a traveler, if you rush around, trying to check things off your list just so you can "say you've been there," you sacrifice real emotional connections with the places you visit. But as a journaler, if you linger too long over your words, attempting to craft bestseller-quality prose, or if you insist on writing down "everything" that happens to you, you'll find yourself overwhelmed, scrambling to keep up as your trip moves forward.

The number one roadblock travel journalers face has nothing to do with good writing. Over and over in my classes, when I ask my students about their past journaling endeavors, the frustration they express most is that they quit writing because they couldn't find time. So before we begin beautifying our words in the next few chapters, let's see if we can do something about this pesky time thing. If you can't find time to write, there's no use learning good writing techniques.

When I was eight years old, living in England, I didn't care whether my writing was good or not. I just wrote. I wasn't trying to be the next Bill Bryson or Paul Theroux. My goal was simply to remember stuff, so I wrote down what I could. By the time I got to college, though, I had grandiose ambitions of getting published. Serious writers, I believed, suffered for their words. Serious writers martyred themselves, laboring for hours to craft the Greatest Sentence Ever. So as I traveled, I would ignore the exciting world around me, and pull out my hair* as I clawed through my mind in search of the perfect way to express myself.

*which I had back then

An hour later, I'd have two paragraphs written. Then it would dawn on me that by spending so much time and energy trying to write about my trip, I was missing my trip. My solution: Slam the notebook shut.

"I'll get back to this later," I'd tell myself.

I rarely got back to it later.

I have a drawer full of unfinished journals from my early 20s. Each contains the first few days of an exciting journey, followed by a pile of blank pages. The days themselves were never blank, but my journals about them are.

I wasn't alone in my journaling meltdowns. People have

them all the time. "I gave up on journaling," people tell me, "because there wasn't enough time to write everything down."

Write down *everything*? What is "everything?"

Everything is infinity.

Try counting to infinity.

Seriously, try it. Ready? Go!

Okay, you can stop now. I'm getting bored.

Here's my point: When you're off on a big adventure, you want to be out *having* that adventure, not sitting around for hours with your nose in your notebook. Even the most dedicated travel journalers are travelers first and journalers second. That's why we must journal quickly and efficiently when we travel. Our time to write is limited.

The challenge here is that most of us have been brainwashed. We've been taught all our lives not to write recklessly. In first or second grade, we were indoctrinated into the Cult of Neat Handwriting. If we wrote quickly and messily, we were scolded. By high school, we were taught to write, and rewrite, and rewrite again in search of the perfect prose that would convince our English teacher he or she had discovered the next Ernest Hemingway. We've carried these ideas with us as we've become free-thinking adults. With such lofty goals, it's no wonder we freeze when so-called "perfection" does not flow effortlessly from our pens.

There is not enough time to write everything down, and there is especially not enough time to write everything down if we are going to try to be "perfect." We have to write fast, and we have to be selective about what we cover.

If you have come home from past trips with mostly empty journals, there are ways to fix this problem, and most people find these solutions not only easy, but liberating. Give yourself permission to write less, and you will actually write more.

Your Former English Teachers Might Hate Me But...

I'm going to teach you a journaling technique that goes against everything you learned in school about how to write. I call it "speed journaling." Some people fall in love with speed journaling the first time they try it. Others take a little while to warm up to the concept, but once they get the hang of it, they make dramatic breakthroughs.

Speed journaling is more efficient than any other journaling method I know. It is by no means the only way to journal, but it's my favorite because it enables us to fill our pages with lots of impressions and stories in a short amount of time. Furthermore, it's a technique we can use in tandem with other journaling methods we'll learn later in this book.

The basic idea behind speed journaling is to splash as much detail onto the page as fast as possible, without wasting time searching for the perfect word, or fretting over punctuation, or worrying whether your handwriting looks sufficiently pretty. On the surface, this might sound like a lousy way to keep a travel journal. We don't want our "ultimate souvenirs" to be a bunch of messy, hastily concocted scrawls. But ask yourself this: Years from now, when you read your old journals, which reaction would you like to have:

> "Wow! All of these pages bring back so many great memories!"
>
> or
>
> "Wow! This journal doesn't tell me much about my trip, but look how totally awesome my spelling and punctuation are in the three paragraphs I did write!"

Time is at a premium when we travel. The ticking clock is like a snarling, fire-breathing dragon. Speed journaling is our proverbial St. George, helping us slay our time dragon. When we don't stop to think about whether our writing is "good enough," when we *just write,* words flow onto the page so much faster. In 10 or 20 minutes, we can blast out a synopsis of our day. When we write slowly, when we attempt to write "well," we often don't write much at all, and what we do write ends up sounding strained, insincere, not like our true voice.

If you want to write exquisitely crafted travel essays, that's great, but exquisitely crafted essays take more time than the time we have during our vacations. So let your travel journals serve as a memory triggers – rough drafts that will bring you back later to the places you've visited, with lots of detail. You can always polish up your words once your trip is over – and that can be a fun way to relive your journeys after they are finished – but while you are traveling, focus on squeezing as many details from your trip onto your pages as quickly as you can. When traveling, a first draft is all we have time to write – and first drafts are not supposed to be perfect.

The bottom line is this: Journal slowly and carefully and you will miss out. You will miss out on lots of details in your journal, and you will miss out on lots of travel experiences because your journaling is taking too much time.

In our next chapter, we'll explore other techniques in which we can slow down our writing if we want. But even if speed journaling sounds like it's not your thing, give it a try. Once people get the hang of it, they're often amazed how much better their journals become. Contrary to what you might expect, many people discover speed journaling makes their writing richer and more exciting. I've even had high school English teachers confess they had no idea how productive this seemingly reckless method of writing can be.

How Speed Journaling Works

Speed journaling is deliciously easy. It will free you from your perfectionism and enable you to write more boldly, more fearlessly, more descriptively than you ever can write if you spend time editing, critiquing, and censoring your thoughts. The basic premise is simple:

Don't think. Just write.

How can you write without thinking? Well, you can't. We are *always* thinking. Our minds are always working. But there's passive thinking and there's perfectionist thinking. Don't stop to worry about whether your writing is good or not. Just keep going.

Speed journaling is based on techniques by creativity gurus Natalie Goldberg and Julia Cameron. Cameron, in her book *The Artist's Way,* describes what she calls "morning pages," in which, first thing in the morning, you fill three notebook pages with whatever tumbles out of your brain and onto paper. The goal is to write so fast that whatever is on your mind gets written down before you have time to decide whether or not it's okay. Cameron suggests that when you do this, you clear the emotional fog from your brain that would otherwise weigh you down throughout the day.

Goldberg, in her groundbreaking books such as *Wild Mind* and *Writing Down the Bones*, teaches us to free ourselves from the fear that way too often leads to writer's block. She offers a technique she calls "timed writing." Timed writing differs from morning pages in that we write, unbridled and uninhibited by self-censorship, for a certain amount of time rather than a certain number of pages. In timed writing, Goldberg explains, you can set whatever time limit you want – five minutes or two hours – but during that time, the idea is to write and write and write, without pausing to worry whether the writing is good or not.

"Lose control," Goldberg urges her readers. "Don't think. Don't get logical. Don't cross out. Don't worry about punctuation, spelling, or grammar." If you get stuck, without any words coming to mind, she suggests freeing yourself with this sentence:

"What I am really trying to say is ________."

"You are free to write the worst junk in America," she tells us. Since we're talking about travel, let's stretch that idea. When speed journaling, you are free to write the worst junk in the world.

"But Dave, I don't want to write junk."

That's the beauty of this no-holds-barred approach. If we allow ourselves to write "junk," we don't. On one touchy-feely sounding level, I would argue no writing is ever junk. Words are simply words, put onto paper in the best way we can translate them from our thoughts. Whether you buy that or not, once you master the art of speed journaling (and most people get it after only one or two quick attempts), you'll find that all sorts of thoughts find their way onto your pages in almost magical ways. Many people are amazed to discover that once they really let go and *just write,* ideas they were keeping buried deep in their subconscious minds begin to reveal themselves. Their words take on an exciting new honesty.

Flight Simulator

Speed Journaling About Journaling

Welcome to your first Flight Simulation! To get a quick taste of how speed journaling works, let's try it out.

In this first exercise, instead of journaling about our travels, let's journal about journaling. For 10 minutes, write anything you want about your thoughts on travel journaling – your goals, your fears, your past experiences, or what you hope to accomplish journaling on an upcoming trip. If you've journaled in the past, you might write about what's gone well in your journaling endeavors, and what hasn't gone so well. How do these things make you feel?

Do this near a timer or a clock. Limit yourself to 10 minutes. Write whatever you can write in that short slice of time. When your time is up, stop. If some of your thoughts haven't made it onto the page yet, that's okay. If they're important, they'll be waiting for you when you pick another time to write. (You can do all of the exercises in this book more than once. Remember, the more you practice, the better your writing becomes.)

But wait! Before we begin, there's an important safety issue I must address. I once had to administer first aid to a lady in a writing class because she developed a horrible hand cramp. Do not let this happen to you – unless there happens to be a really cute person in your immediate vicinity from whom you would like to receive first aid. Speed journaling, as the name suggests, is about writing fast, but it's about writing fast in a mental and emotional sense, not in a physical sense. This isn't supposed to be painful!

Before you begin, take a moment to center yourself. Breathe deeply. Scan the muscle groups in your body, beginning with your head and face, slowly moving downward through your shoulders and arms, your back, your torso, your legs, and into your toes. Where you feel tension, try to relax. This is important. When we are in a hurry, we get tense, and that tension can clog our writing. Speed journaling isn't a race. It's a freeing of the mind. It's allowing our thoughts to pour out of us naturally.

So relax. Open your notebook and get ready to write. Remember the exercise: Journal for 10 minutes about journaling. As you write, don't forget to breathe. When your time is up, continue reading.

Hidden Thoughts

Often when we speed journal, thoughts that we didn't know were there bubble to the surface of our minds. There are all sorts of things we passively recognize about ourselves but never put into words. Writers often have fears that hold them back. In the exercise we just did – writing about writing – those fears might make themselves known. Did any of the following ideas show up in your speed journaling exercise? (Or have any of them crossed your mind at other times?):

- I'm afraid to write what I really think because someone else might read it.
- I want to write, but when I sit down to do it, I don't feel like writing.
- Even though I'm not "supposed" to feel this way when speed journaling, I'm afraid my writing won't be "good enough."
- I've tried travel journaling before and I've failed. What if I just can't do it?
- I'm afraid to write about certain things because they might stir up old emotions or issues I don't want to deal with – especially in the middle of a fun vacation.
- I have bigger issues in my life right now than journaling. That's what I should be focusing my time and energy on.
- Is the phone about to ring and interrupt me? I'm hungry. Do my feet smell?

Maybe you had one or more of these thoughts. Maybe you had all of them. Maybe you had none of them. Regardless, if you were able to write steadily and honestly, you have succeeded in your first speed journaling endeavor. (And if you didn't manage to write down certain thoughts in this exercise, that's okay too. You might not have gotten to them in this limited amount of time, or you might have avoided them because they made you uncomfortable. Don't worry about that for now. We'll learn to handle these mental blocks a little later.)

The rest of the exercises in this book will focus on writing about travel, not writing about writing. In the coming chapters, you'll discover other benefits to speed journaling. Hopefully this first exercise has taught you something about your journaling goals, beliefs, hesitations, and the things that might be holding you back from your best writing.

One thing I love about speed journaling is it strips away our desire to "sound like a writer." It's natural and non-pretentious. It's the real us, our true voice. Many people find that once they get the hang of speed journaling, their writing becomes more sincere, more fearless, because they stop censoring themselves and holding back certain thoughts. Regardless, speed journaling gives you more time to enjoy your travels. In a 10-minute writing blitz, you can cover all the highlights of your day. Then you can go out and have more highlights.

Contrary to popular belief, great writing is not nearly as much a "gift" as it is a learnable skill. The more you practice, the better you will get. With more polished forms of writing, this improvement shows as we revise our work and mold our words just as we want them. With speed journaling, the more you do it, the more relaxed you will become, and the more detail you'll be able to splash onto the page.

Dave's Diaries

Dubrovnik, Croatia

I always travel with a pocket-sized notebook. It is my to-do list, my depository for random facts, a reminder of freelance article ideas I might pursue later, my temporary phone book, and if things get really dull, material for the construction of miniature paper airplanes. (I have never actually had to resort to the mini airplanes.) On occasion, it also becomes my makeshift journal, if my main journal is back at my hotel or otherwise not in my possession.

Last summer, on a break between tours I was guiding, I caught up with my friend and travel writing colleague, Pat O'Connor, in Croatia. On our first full day, we took a break at the top of a bluff that overlooked the Adriatic Sea. We were in a serene setting that, not so long ago, had been a war zone.

I pulled out my pocket notebook, and did a quick writing blast, coupling Speed Journaling with a technique called "Verbal Shapshots" that I'll teach you in the next chapter. For five minutes, I wrote down whatever I saw around me.

That quick scribble, which filled only one tiny page, captured the basic details of the scene and the thoughts in my head. It became a springboard for a more detailed entry in my blog about both the physical landscape around me and the mental landscape in my brain.

As a professional writer, I often spend more time journaling than most travelers, polishing my words as I go. Once I had my initial blurb written, I took another 30 or 40 minutes developing it into an essay for my blog. You can do this too if you like -- polish up your words while you travel, or once you're home and have more time. Or you can skip the rewriting. Either way, your on-the-road record of a few quick details will be enough to spark your memories once your trips are finished.

Here now are both my initial Speed Journaling blast, and the more detailed article that followed.

A Deeper Kind of Laughter

The Speed Journal:

Pat and I have just climbed a steep hill on an asphalt road that seemed to amplify the sun as it echoed off the road. I'm gooey with sweat. Luckily we found beer. So I'm in this outdoor café now, with a white awning of corrugated plastic for shade. "Footloose" by Kenny Loggins is playing on the radio. Kenny Loggins? Come on! I thought Croatia had caught up with the rest of Europe. I'm drinking a bottle of Amstel, looking out over the coast, with an eerie feeling. Way down below us, a few hundred feet, is the sea – bright turquoise waters splashing up on a dry coastline. It's beautiful and peaceful and serene. It's hard to believe people were killing each other here a decade ago – shooting, bombing, destroying. It's an uncomfortable contrast – this idyllic beauty, and the knowledge of what happened.

The Polished Essay:

I'm sitting at an outdoor café, nursing a beer. Kenny Loggins is belting out "Footloose" on a local radio station, but other than that, life is pretty good here.

The sun is sweltering, pounding down through humid air. I like heat and humidity. It's as if the air is giving you one of those smothering hugs you received as a child from some eccentric, over-perfumed relative. Down below me, the Adriatic Sea is spooning a dry, tree-cluttered coastline.

This feels idyllic. And I feel confused.

I feel confused because I'm a humor writer – and specifically, a travel humor writer whenever possible. I'm sitting in this idyllic place, unable to shake from my head the thought that 15 years ago, bombs were raining down upon this town that today feels innocent and safe.

I'm confused because I have learned over the years that humor is born out of incongruities. Squish two ideas together that don't really fit, create surprise and confusion, and *voilà*! People laugh. But I'm feeling *massive* incongruity here, between the war that happened, and the serenity today, and I can't find humor in it.

I will say this: I feel happy here. I feel happy because logically, I get what happened a decade and a half ago, but after a night and a morning in this vacation town, I'm not seeing evidence of the war. Two-thirds of the buildings in Dubrovnik were damaged when the Serbs attacked in 1991, but there is little evidence today, other than a lot of construction and the occasional building scarred by what might or might not be bullet holes. If you look harder, you can find more evidence; the tiles on the roofs are all brand new. But the people of Dubrovnik have done an amazing job of rebuilding, recovering, and moving on.

At first glance, it's hard for a naïve outsider like me to understand why anyone would attack Dubrovnik. According to my taxi driver yesterday, only 47,000 people live here. According to my guidebook, the Serbs attacked to cripple the tourism industry – to sting economically and emotionally by striking at what my part-time employer, Rick Steves, describes as Croatia's "proudest, most historic, and most beautiful city, the tourist capital of a nation dependent on tourism."

At first glance, it is difficult to find humor in incongruity here. But I'm finding something better. I am finding smiles, and laughter – not laughter at snarky jokes like the kind I tend to come up with, but deeper, alive laughter among the people who live here, who seem once again happy. Today in Dubrovnik, the only source of oppression is an overzealous sun. Life as it should be has returned.

It would be naïve and insensitive of me to think there

are no emotional scars from a complex war in which innocent civilians on *all* sides were hurt. But people around me seem calm and content once again – proof that people can and do bounce back from traumas.

Fifteen years later, Dubrovnik is again a vibrant city, a place where life is celebrated. It gives me hope that innocent civilians in current war zones might also laugh again one day.

CHAPTER 3

Journaling Outside the Box

Creative Techniques for Super-Journalers

Most people approach their journals in simple chronological order: morning, afternoon, evening, next day, day after that, lather, rinse, repeat. It's an easy way to organize everything. You've got a ready-made, no-brain-required outline, so you don't have to spend lots of time organizing your thoughts.

Excellent! I'm all for effort-free, slacker techniques, as long as they work. Just be careful. Writing this way has a potentially monstrous pitfall: Our words can bog down with flabby details. As the flab congeals, we run out of breath and our journals collapse.

Cover the Highlights. Cut the Flab.

If you've fretted in the past that your writing was boring, the tone of the following paragraph might sound familiar:

> *Today I woke up early. I had a croissant and coffee at the hotel. Then I went to see the Eiffel Tower. Paris was beautiful. Then I walked around the Champs Elysées. I found a*

> *nice café for lunch. I had a ham and cheese baguette. Then I went to the Louvre. It was so amazing to see the Mona Lisa. After the Louvre, I caught the metro back to the hotel. My feet hurt. Blah, blah, blah...blah, blah, blah, blah.*

All too often, journals fall flat. They're bland, step-by-step accounts of our day: "I went here. Then I went here. Then I did this. Then I...."

Yawn.

They become pedestrian. There's no emotion. In trying to write about "everything" that happens, we pad our big adventures with a whole bunch of boring stuff.

If you watch a movie about an event that happened over the course of a year, is the movie a year long? Of course not. Producers condense the highlights into a couple of hours. That's how our journals should be too. Pick three or four highlights each day and let go of other events. Whatever you had for breakfast is probably boring and does not warrant space in your journal, unless it was something exciting like a feta-and-rhinoceros omelet.* That would be worth writing about. But a croissant? Ask yourself if that is really journal-worthy, compared with more exciting stuff you've done that day.

*In hollandaise sauce. Yum!

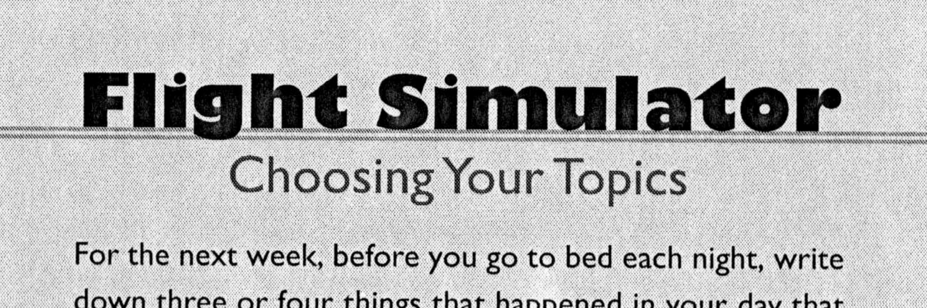

Flight Simulator

Choosing Your Topics

For the next week, before you go to bed each night, write down three or four things that happened in your day that you consider journal-worthy. If you can only come up with one or two topics, that's fine, but do not exceed four.

Once you make your list each night, ask yourself if

each topic is something you could cover in five minutes or less. If they are…great. If not, you have two choices:

Look at any potentially lengthy topics and decide what key points you could cover in three to five minutes, or...

If you have written something down that you really would need more time to write about, cross other topics off of your list to create more time for the big one.

After you've whittled your list down to a manageable size, you can journal about these items if you like. Unless you are doing this exercise during a journey in progress, however, if you don't have time to actually journal about the things on your list, that's fine. The idea here is simply to practice looking at your day and deciding what's most important to write about.

With practice, you'll be able to do the above exercise quickly in your head and then dive right into your journaling. For the first week, however, write your list down so you can look at it and really consider whether it's realistic.

Once you've done this for a week, you might like to continue doing this same exercise in your head each night. Doing so, you'll become more adept at choosing topics quickly when traveling – and this exercise can also bring some closure or reflection to your days at home if you're not keeping an actual diary.

Alternative Techniques

Let's shake things up now and look beyond this most common approach to journaling. We're going to be rebels and journal outside the box. If this scares you, if you are not a natural born rebel, trust me. These techniques won't hurt you. They're what the cool kids are doing these days…and they're all safe and legal.

That having been said, please approach the rest of this chapter in moderation. I'm about to throw a whole bunch of new stuff at you. Lots of ideas. Lots of exercises. You don't have to attempt them all in one sitting. You can if you want to, but if you experience any dizziness, drowsiness, sweating, twitching, irritability, or other side effects, take a break. Take a walk, take a nap, have a coffee, have a beer...call time out and put this book aside for a little while. I'll still be here when you come back; I promise.

You can pursue all of these techniques in tandem with speed journaling if you like. You could also, however, slow down your writing and see what happens. If you're short on time, speed journal as you travel, then polish things up later.

Theme Journaling

Suspend your sense of time for a moment. What if you didn't write in a linear, chronological fashion? What if you bounced, semi-haphazardly, from journey to journey as you wrote? You'd be kind of like a time traveler, only without ever having to hang out with mad scientists, who tend to get annoying.

You can do that! You can cast aside the hour-by-hour, day-by-day, journey-by-journey structure of your journals and leap around, writing about multiple trips in a single journal entry! How do you do this without sounding like a ranting lunatic? By finding an alternate structure, a different thread that ties your words together – a theme!

What sorts of themes do we encounter in our travels that differ from our everyday routines? Food, weather, money, language, transportation, accommodations, showers, animals, luggage, telephones, chocolate, music, news, other travelers, gardens, health, water, safety, smells, pickpockets, children, art, noise, religion, beer, e-mail, shopping, haggling, ticket lines, more chocolate, and iguanas, to name a few. In all, there are approximately 79 trillion different travel themes, give or take, for you to write about. Many of these themes are universal; we encounter them no matter where we go. Others might be location-specific: folk music in Ireland, sushi in Japan, siestas in Mexico, or witches in Oz, to name a few.

Cover a different theme each day. Zero in on the unique parts of your journey. If you choose to write about food on day twelve of your trip, you might have memorable stories to tell from days two, six, and nine. Write as much detail as you can about a specific topic rather than the broader events of a specific moment.

You don't need to stick to your current journey either. Say you're traveling in Scotland and you decide to write about foreign accents. You can write one journal entry about accents you've encountered on various trips to Scotland, Jamaica, Chicago, Texas, and Kiribati. Perhaps in Paris, a chocolate mousse sends you on a writing binge about dessert. So write too about the baklava you had in Greece, the flan you ate in Brazil, and the apple pie you had in Kalamazoo.

If your travels tend closer to home, you'll find plenty of themes across your own country. In the United States, for example, you might write about highway rest stops, varying moralities or politics in different places, vehicles, airports, or odd local cuisines.

Do this long enough and you've written yourself a fun book of essays that criss-cross your journeys, lacing together your lifetime of travel experiences and impressions.

Flight Simulator

Choosing Your Themes

Make a list of themes you'd like to journal about. Brainstorm for five to ten minutes. There's no such thing as a bad theme. If something pops into your head, even if it seems ridiculous, write it down. When you think you've run out of themes, sit quietly for a few more minutes. Often the best themes are the ones that come to you after you have emptied the obvious ones out of your mind and onto paper.

Once you've made your list of themes, choose one and write about it in regard to your past travels. It can be a theme covering lots of different trips, or you can focus on one specific journey.

Hang onto your list. Bring it along when you travel, and add to it whenever something jumps into your head. You'll have a ready-made list of topics to write about as you explore.

(And for a longer list of my favorite journaling themes, visit my website at **www.traveljournaling.com**.)

People Journaling

Travel boldly and you'll always cross paths with fascinating strangers. You might engage in lengthy conversations, or you might never speak a word to them. Either way, the people whose lives intersect your itineraries can make for fascinating writing. Choose one person each day as you travel and describe your encounter.

Scrutinize people a little when you first meet them. Don't be creepy about it, but take a good, stealthy look. Make mental notes. It will help you recall details later. What are they wearing? Is their skin soft and smooth, or rough and weathered? Does anything about their physical appearance stand out? A scar? A birthmark? An unusual haircut? A facial tic? Can you detect emotion in their eyes? Joy? Fatigue? Curiosity? Indifference? How about lustful desire?* What about their hair? Their hands? Their nose? Their knees? Their...(insert favorite body part here).

*You sexy thing, you!

Take this a step further. Go beyond the surface physical description. How do they speak? Fast or slow? Loud or soft? Do they have an accent or use unusual local expressions? When it's time to write, put their words in quotes, and try to write those quotes the way *they* spoke, not the way you speak. It doesn't matter if you can't remember their words verbatim. You're not writing for *The New York Times* here. It's your private journal. Nobody's going to sue you if you don't quote them perfectly. Just come as close as you can. The way someone speaks reveals all kinds of things about his or her personality, education, social class, ethnicity, and so on.

(If, however, you do plan to publish your journals later, it then becomes very important to quote people accurately if they are mentioned by name or otherwise identifiable.)

Also keep in mind that language goes beyond the words that leave our mouths. Don't forget people's mannerisms. Did they gesture with their hands or scrunch their brow? Was their posture confident or meek? Did they smile? Were they stone-faced? All of these details help capture the personality of a newfound friend in a faraway place or a stranger whose path we might have crossed for just a moment.

How about your impression of them? Why did you have that impression? Do you think your impression was accurate, or was it tinted by something in your own belief system, something from your own culture? What do you think this person was thinking? How did you feel in their presence? What do you imagine their life is like? Why did you notice this person in the first place?

Even fleeting encounters can make for fascinating stories. I can recall dozens of people throughout my travels with whom I never spoke, or with whom I had the briefest of encounters – chatty bus drivers, surly shopkeepers, border guards, beggars, wide-eyed babies in strollers, and other travelers. Sometimes, somebody catches our eye for reasons we're not quite sure of. And sometimes, someone catches our eye for reasons that are very clear. They might look friendly, menacing, interesting, lost, or drop-dead gorgeous. Pick one of these people each day, and write them to life in the pages of your journal.

Flight Simulator

People Spotting

For the next couple of days, keep a list of people you encounter who you don't know. It can be anybody – cashiers or bus drivers, people you meet for the first time at work or school, servers or customers in a restaurant, or simply strangers you pass on the street but never talk to.

Once you have a list of five or more people, choose one and write about him or her for at least 10 minutes. Describe him or her in as much detail as possible and don't forget to explore ideas such as how this person made you feel, why you think you had these feelings, and so on.

Verbal Snapshots

You want to go out and play, but you haven't written in a while. What to do, what to do? I have a solution. I call it the "verbal snapshot."

Choose a place you'd like to go hang out. Bring your notebook and start writing – reporting live from the scene.

Sit at a sidewalk café, sip a cappuccino, and describe the world that swirls around you – the wait staff, other customers, strangers who scurry by on the street.

Find a bench in a museum. Describe the art, and the people who have come to see it.

Get out in nature, someplace secluded and serene, and write about the scene around you and how you feel.

Hang out at the beach, wriggle your toes into the sand, and describe the waves, the seagulls, the local swimsuit fashions.*

With verbal snapshots, as opposed to photographic snapshots, you're never limited to your sense of sight. Write about the sounds that surround you, the smells in the air. Write about how your body feels. Record what you're thinking as you sit and experience the moment.

*Unless you are at a nude beach, in which case you can instead describe the...oh, I can't write that in this book. But you can journal about it! And writing in your journal in this situation is safer that whipping out your camera!

You can write a verbal snapshot just about anywhere – historic sights, restaurants, natural settings, train or bus stations, on trains or buses, even standing on a random street corner. Want a beer? (I do!) Go write in a pub! Get creative in choosing a place to go write each day. If you find you like this journaling style, carry a pocket-sized notebook, separate from your primary journal, specifically for writing down your verbal snapshots. You'll always have it with you, and it's small enough to support with the palm of your hand when a flat writing surface isn't available.

Verbal snapshots focus intensely on a single moment in our travels. They capture a sense of immediacy. Unlike every other form of journaling, there is no time lag between when the event happened and when we wrote it down. We're reporting live from our trip, covering events as they happen around and within us. When we go back and read our snapshots later, our words bring us back to the exact moment when we had the experience.

Flight Simulator

Live Reporting

For practice, pick a place near to wherever you are right

now, and go write about it. Choose a spot in your neighborhood where you like to hang out, or go on a mini road trip for an hour or a day. Limit your writing to whatever is happening around you and within you in that moment.

Captioning

I was guiding a tour in Scandinavia recently and found myself with a free night in Copenhagen. I went to visit my friend, Britta. Britta was cooking dinner for her neighbors. She invited me to stay and pilfer food.

Britta is my parents' age, five feet tall if she really stretches, and a dangerous woman to drink with. She has a guise of innocence, and a sneaky way of buying "just one more round," over and over, until you know it will be painful at work the next morning.

As we sat in Britta's courtyard, she plied us all with wine, and then told her neighbors about my interest in travel journaling. She did so with an ulterior motive. She wanted her neighbor, Malene, to show me her diary from a recent trip to the Caribbean.

Malene hesitated until Britta refilled our wine glasses one more time. The next thing I knew, I was paging through one of the most colorful journals I'd ever seen. Malene's journal consisted of hastily scribbled thoughts that popped into her head as she traveled. Accompanying them were little sketches – drawn with a ballpoint pen, then colored with magic markers. These sketches were not earth-shattering artistic masterpieces. They were quick and simple scribbles – of palm trees, the bungalow where she slept, a fruity drink with the beach in the background, and so on. They added bursts of color and turned her journal into a whimsical work of art.

Malene's journal wasn't *just* a sketch book. Surrounding her cocktail on the beach were a few sentences about what was in the drink, where she was when she ordered it, who served it to her, and how she felt as she slurped it down after an exhausting day of hiking.

If drawing or water-coloring isn't your thing, you can caption photographs too. Digital cameras make this easy, since you can review your photos as you go, and pick a favorite one to write about. If you want to caption photos rather than sketches, leave space in your notebook so you can paste the pictures in once you print or develop them. Before leaving home, decide on a standard size for photos to include in your journal. You might bring one photo of that size with you as a guide to trace around. When you're ready to caption a photograph, section off a spot on the page where you'll add the photo later. If working with a digital image, you can also note the file number from your camera. That way, when you go to paste the picture into your journal later, you'll be sure you get the right one.

Around that space, journal about the photo – not just about what's in it, but also what was happening around you as you took it, the thoughts or emotions that went through your mind, challenges you might have experienced capturing the image, and any other details that aren't obvious from looking at the photograph, such as your other senses, descriptions of people in the photo, or things that were happening "behind the scenes."

Other great things to caption around are all the scraps of paper we accumulate when we travel – transportation tickets, brochures, candy wrappers, business cards, even small denominations of local currency. Buy a glue stick and paste them into your journal. A bus ticket can be a launching pad for a quick description of a local bus ride – what the bus looked like, confusion you encountered buying tickets, people on board, etc. A hotel business card could launch into a description of a memorable hotelier, or the view from your room.

A Postcard a Day

One of the things I dread when I fly home from a long trip is the stack of bills and junk mail that awaits me. You can sweeten this looming pile of depression by sending yourself a postcard every day. You'll come home to lots of little souvenirs waiting in your mailbox…and perhaps a few trickling in over the next week or two.

Buy yourself a postcard each day and write a note to yourself about the place you're visiting. To save time, bring pre-printed labels with your home address. In the end, you'll have not only a collection of quick journal entries, but photos as well, of the places you've been.

As an alternative to mailing the cards home, if you don't feel like searching for stamps in each location, just buy a postcard each day and carry them all home with you. This gives you twice as much room to write since your words can spill over into the address space.

Either way, the beauty of postcard journaling is there's a finite amount of space to guarantee you can't try to write "everything." Just jot down a few quick sentences. And always finish with a loving note to yourself: "Having a great time! Wish you were here!"

Five a Day

If you are *really* struggling to write each day, here's something absolutely everyone can find time for: five sentences a day. Don't think. Write the first five things about your day that come to mind. You will not get the depth of journaling you achieve from other techniques, but if you've been struggling on some days to get anything written, this is a quick way to make sure you write *something* every day. At the end of a two-week trip, you'll have a nice overview of where you've been – and thoughts to trigger other memories when you look back on your trip.

Once you sit down to write your five sentences, more

thoughts might start coming. When that happens, go for it! But if you commit to a five-sentence-a-day journal, remember that writing longer on one day doesn't mean you have to stretch your quota every day. Don't beat yourself up if you don't exceed your goal. And *don't* be perfectionistic about your five sentences. (Perfectionism might very well be what is keeping you from writing a lengthier journal.) Get in the habit of your five-sentence minimum.

In time, many people who do this find their writing takes off into longer entries. When I journal this way, I make it a ritual. I make it the last thing I do before bed, or the first thing I do in the morning.

Group Journaling

If you're traveling with other people, bring one journal for everyone to share. If you have several people contributing to a group project, *you* don't have to write every day. If you're traveling in a group of four, for example, you only journal on every fourth day. Yay for delegating!

Since you'll be sharing your journal, at least among your fellow travelers, you might not document the full scope of thoughts and emotions you'd reveal in a private journal, but as a trade-off, you'll capture the thoughts, perceptions, and personalities of everyone in your posse. You can do this in tandem with just one travel partner, or if you're in a larger group, pass it around to anyone who's interested.

There are also fun ways to ensure everyone writes on their assigned day. Agree ahead of time that anyone who doesn't write when they're supposed to buys dinner for the rest of you. Or find some other motivating penalty that works for your travel companions.

When you get home, photocopy, or type and print your journal for each traveler.

Audio Journals

What about a spoken word journal – with a tape recorder or digital voice recorder? People ask me that a lot. Personally, I don't like to journal this way.

I also do not like karaoke, raisins, or cleaning my kitchen, however. That doesn't make these things evil. Some people find these things quite lovely.* If you want to try audio journaling, by all means, do! Allow me to explain, however, my misgivings.

*If you would like to come over and clean my kitchen, you are welcome to.

I've never been able to ad-lib a recorded journal without losing my train of thought. In addition, technology can bite you. Batteries die. Files crash. Tapes snarl. A lot less can go wrong with a pen and paper.

The biggest reason I don't like recorded journals is I never listen to them once I get home. For me, there's something simpler about flipping open a notebook for a peek than there is to finding a spot in a recording, pressing play, and listening to my own voice ramble on. My mind wanders. I get distracted and stop paying attention to myself. With my written journals, I can skim through them quickly.

All of this having been said, there are fun things you can do with a voice recorder that you can't do on paper – interview your travel partner, capture ambient sound from the world around you, or sing late-night hotel room karaoke. If you are dying to try a recorded journal, you have my blessing. You might not have the problems I have. Unlike me, perhaps you have the attention span of an adult.

A Story a Day

It's time to wrap up this chapter with an adaptation of the day-by-day, chronological journaling style we discussed earlier. Remember what I suggested a few pages ago? If you go with the most common, linear format, choose three or four significant events in your day rather than skimming the surface of everything. Now, let's take that idea to an extreme. Instead of slimming your day down to three or four significant moments, you get only one.

"But Dave, I do more than one cool thing a day when I travel!"

I certainly hope so. That's not the point.

Traveling to me is about collecting stories. I'm always looking for anecdotes I can publish, or at least fling out to the world on my blog in a nicely packaged morsel. That's one reason I personally like this approach. In Chapter 9, we'll look at taking your journals public – writing stories that (1) you want to share, and (2) other people want to read. But even if you're not interested in sharing your journals with others, give this a try. Focus on a single event each day – an anecdote that's fun, eye-opening, or inspiring. Write one anecdote each day on a two-week trip, and you'll return home with a fun collection of 14 stories about 14 things that happened along the way.

Which Technique Is Best?

Which of these techniques is best? That's your call. Find what works for you. Mix and match these techniques from day to day, or devote a trip to one specific style. Experiment. See what you like best. There's no single right or wrong way to journal. The most effective styles for you are usually the ones you enjoy the most. Find an approach you like and you'll be more likely to stick to it.

Try new things too. You might concoct other earth-shattering techniques that are even cooler than these. If you do, I'd love to hear from you! You can reach me through my website at **traveljournaling.com**.

Dave's Diaries

Reykjavík, Iceland (People Journaling)

The people we meet while traveling sometimes become some of our most significant memories. And sometimes, a person can have a big impact on us even though we never actually meet him or her. A fleeting glance can be powerful, and journal-worthy.

In 1989, just hours into my three-month trip around Europe, I passed a young woman on the streets of Reykjavík. We never spoke, but her memory still haunts me.

Shivers

I wandered into a residential neighborhood, away from the shops and traffic. As I walked, I spotted a young woman, around my age, coming toward me. Her features were Icelandic, but like me, she was not properly dressed. She wore a thin cotton dress that clung tight against her skin when the wind blew. She was clutching herself for warmth. She was shivering, and squinting in discomfort. As she moved closer to me, I allowed myself to do something I rarely do. I let my eyes lock with hers.

It wasn't the flirtatious glance you might think. It was curiosity maybe, or concern, or a shared sense of loneliness. She looked very sad.

Our eyes remained locked as we passed each other. Our heads turned to prolong the gaze. I couldn't tell whether the tears that dampened the sides of her eyelids were from the wind or from crying, but she had a pleading expression. I wanted to say something, to ask if I could help in some way, but intimidated by the language barrier, I stayed silent. Eventually, we both turned our heads forward and kept going.

As I walked away, I realized the self-induced loneliness I was feeling at the beginning of a solo journey was nothing to fret over. My life was good, void of the personal worry that seemed to be weighing on this other troubled soul. I'll never know her story. She was just some person I passed on the street – one random human on our planet of six billion.

Dave's Diaries

Vancouver, British Columbia, Canada (Verbal Snapshots)

On a recent weekend getaway in Canada, I found myself face-to-face with a very curious black squirrel in Vancouver's Stanley Park. I thought the squirrel would flee as soon as I reached for the little hand-held notebook I always carry, but he didn't. He watched as I began writing. Perhaps he was in awe of my Travel Journaling Superhero aura; I'm not sure.

In any event, I stood in the park and spent 10 minutes speed-journaling a verbal snapshot. A few days later, home in Seattle, I spent another 10 minutes polishing up my words.

Squirrel Watching in Stanley Park

There's a black squirrel staring straight at me as I write this. He's hanging out by my feet, looking up with beady eyes, waiting for a snack.

I have no snack to give him, and if I did, I probably shouldn't. I've never been this close to a wild squirrel before. As we stare at each other, I realize I am communicating with a wild animal in some strange way. I am wondering: Why is it that we consider squirrels cute, but rats atrocious? The squirrel's bushy tail must have something to do with it.

My squirrel eventually gets bored watching me write. He runs off into a nearby swamp.

There's a man standing about 50 feet from me. I have yet to communicate with him. He seems a little eccentric. He's trying to feed the birds – trying to get them to land on his hand and peck from his palm. The birds, however, are heard, not seen. I can hear all kinds of species chirping in the woods around me, but none of them trust the man.

None will come in for a landing or a meal. The squirrels, on the other hand, seem fearless. Eight of them are surrounding the man, hoping for a handout. The man is ignoring the squirrels. He is trying not to move. He looks very serious.

An airplane flies overhead, its drone breaking the sounds of nature. I wonder what the squirrels think when they hear an airplane. They don't react. They don't seem frightened. But what do they think the plane is? Do they even notice the sound? They must.

And what do they think of us humans?

Another squirrel scampers off the trail, into the swamp where I won't walk. I can't skip across tree roots and keep my feet dry.

I watch the squirrel disappear under a bush. I hear him dash into his unseen world that begins just feet away from me. Off the path, deep in the bushes, these squirrels have a culture of their own, a community, a microcosm, an entire way of life I will never get to visit.

CHAPTER 4

The Outer Journey

Capturing the Scene

OW that you've learned how to write without letting your journals gobble up your precious time, and you've tried some nifty new techniques, let's hit the road!

In the next few chapters, we'll look at the two halves of every journey – your outer journey and your inner journey.

I know, I know. Some people are going to roll their eyes and think, "Inner journey? Do we have to dress up in sheets and sell books at the airport and play tambourines?"

No. You do not have to dress up in sheets unless you think you look devilishly gorgeous in them. You do not have to sell anything at the airport.* And you can skip the tambourine unless you are looking to start a Partridge Family cover band. I promise not to get over-the-top, new-agey here.

What do I mean by your "outer journey" and your "inner journey?" Oh, you're a smart person. You've probably figured it out already – at least in part – but allow me to elaborate.

Your outer journey is your stage, so to speak. It's everything

*Though you are free to recommend my books to friendly-looking people.

that surrounds you when you travel. It encompasses all of your senses – what you see, hear, smell, taste, and feel (in terms of physical touch). It also includes where you go, what you do, whom you meet, and so on. The outer journey is the framework for your travel journal.

Your inner journey is made up of everything that goes on in your head as you travel – your thoughts, plans, hopes, anxieties, and the intimidating yet scrumptious confusion we call "culture shock." Whenever you leave your usual world and venture into unfamiliar places, those places stretch your mind in ways it doesn't get stretched at home. Writing about your inner journey as you travel can spark big insights about yourself.

If you've journaled while traveling before, which of your two journeys have you focused on the most? Most people fixate on their outer journey and neglect the inner one. But when we travel, especially in distant cultures (and as we'll learn in Chapter 6, distant cultures don't necessarily have to be far from home), we tend to get so wrapped up in the different world around us, we forget to write about our feelings and emotions. Our inner journey is often the most powerful part of a trip.

In the next few chapters, we'll explore these two parallel journeys, and learn how to integrate them in our writing. Weaving the two together brings depth to your journals. In this chapter, we'll begin with the outer journey.

Scanning Your Senses, Picturing the Scene

Before you start writing about your outer journey, take a moment to picture yourself back in the scene you want to cover. This brings the day's details to the forefront of your mind. Close your eyes if you like.* Recall the events of your day. As you do this, scan through each of your senses – sight, sound, smell, taste, and touch.

We've got five senses, but they're not equal. The focus of our senses shifts from situation to

*If you are jetlagged, however, be careful not to start snoring.

situation. Ponder for a moment which of your five senses would be the dominant ones in the following situations:

- Spotting a rainbow from a moving train
- Wandering through a spice market
- Eating a gooey, chocolate dessert
- Going to a concert
- Watching a fireworks display
- Splashing in an icy stream

You might have come up with more than one answer for some of the above scenarios. For all of them, you were probably able to quickly identify one or two senses that stood out above the others, and those one or two dominant senses most likely varied from one situation to the next.

Our dominant sense in any given situation often seems like the most important one, and there's a tendency to ignore or simply not notice the others. But when we fail to check out the other senses, we risk missing big details. This is why it's so important to do a quick scan of *all* of your senses – not just the ones that stand out the strongest.

Before you begin writing, imagine yourself back in the moment you are going to journal about and ask yourself all of the following questions:

- What do I see?
- What do I hear?
- What do I smell?
- What do I taste?
- What do I feel?

In the context of the outer journey, that last question, "What do I feel?" means "feel" in the physical sense, not the emotional sense. Are you hot or cold? Relaxed or tense? Sleepy? Over-caffeinated? Are your feet sore from too much walking? (And is that soreness good or bad? Sometimes at the end of a long day, aching feet can feel strangely blissful. They prove we've really been out exploring.)

Among the other four questions – what do you see, hear, smell, and taste? – some can be trickier than others to answer. What we see is usually easy to write about. In a quiet place, on the other hand, we might think we hear nothing. But stop and listen for a moment. Even when things are silent, there's usually still some subtle sound. As I pause from typing this chapter in a "quiet room," I hear the soft whirr of my computer, and the buzz of a lamp behind me. There's the barely audible drone of traffic a block away. And, hey, there goes an airplane overhead. Try sitting in a completely quiet room sometime and notice what you hear. You may be surprised how many sounds exist among "silence."

Smell and taste can be even more subtle – or they can dominate what's around us. If we're scarfing down that gooey, chocolate dessert, our sense of taste might be blissfully dominant.* But when you're not eating, can you taste anything? Maybe it's the coffee you had earlier in the day, or unusual spices that have lingered after an exotic meal, or the minty flavor of freshly brushed teeth. And smells? Some smells are potent, easy to notice and easy to describe. Others are much more subtle. Can you smell anything around you right now? When you journal, pay close attention to the subtleties. How, for example, does the air in a museum smell compared to the air on a city street or the air on a beach? You may also notice that subtle scents become more noticeable in a place you return to from time to time. In my early 20s, I went back to visit the elementary school in England where I spent third grade. As I

*If on the other hand, chocolate makes you break out in hives, what you feel might overtake what you taste once the itching kicks in.

walked through the courtyard, I was immediately engulfed in the scent of a particular tree that stood outside the school. I don't remember what kind of tree it was, but it had a distinct smell, a smell I hadn't smelled in years. The scent of the tree brought a flood of memories rushing back.

Why is it so important to scan *all* of the senses? Because depending on our situation, dominant senses can overpower more subtle ones – but those more subtle senses often tell stories of their own.

Spicy Sounds

A few years ago, I went wandering through a Turkish spice bazaar. Which senses would dominate such a setting? Obviously smell, with the unusual aromas from hundreds of spices, mingling together and wafting into the air. And sight – the colors – bold yet earthy shades of red, yellow, and green, each representing a different spice on display, side by side in big baskets, creating a feast for the eyes as well as the nose.

Those are the two senses that dominated my thoughts as I walked through the spice market. But once I started thinking about what I could hear, I picked up on two snippets of Turkish culture that I never would have noticed if I hadn't scanned through my senses and paid attention to the sounds.

As I strolled through the market, I noticed a soft clinking sound rising just above the drone of the spice vendors who were trying to lure customers to their stalls. The sound came and went, fading in and out of the cacophony of voices, and I began to wonder what it was. Eventually I realized it was what the Turks call "tea boys" – kids who worked in the market – carrying metal trays that hung from handles, decked with little shot glasses of tea for the merchants. Tea is a national obsession in Turkey. More than just a caffeinated beverage, it's a social tool, a reason to sit and chat, a quick break from work. This subtle sound provided the basis for a fun journal entry about Turkey's love for tea.

Two other sounds entered my mind as I paused to think. They were sounds that might have jumped out at some travelers right away, but having spent some time in Turkey, neither struck me as noteworthy at first, and I almost neglected to write them down. One of those sounds was the call to prayer – a crackly burst of loudspeaker static from the minaret atop a mosque, followed by an imam bellowing, "*Allahu akhbar*" – "God is great. Come and pray," inviting the neighborhood to join in the Muslim custom of praying five times daily.

As the prayer call echoed through the bazaar, so did Madonna. Her latest CD was blaring from a boom box in one of the spice sellers' stalls. In this liberal part of Istanbul, prayer calls still wafted from the mosques five times daily, but they often went ignored, drowned out by business transactions and the love some Turks have for Western pop music.

This image of Madonna and the imam competing for attention in a crowd of people painted a potent picture of the rift that divides Turkey today. Some devout Muslims are calling for a return to the old ways, when Islam played a more substantial role in everyday life. Other Turks are itching to Westernize, to become part of modern Europe, and to adopt Western culture. The prayer call and the American pop music juxtaposed in such a way were symbolic of the two directions in which Turkey is feeling tugged. Neither of those two sounds had anything to do with spices, but if I hadn't stopped to notice them, filling my ears simultaneously, I would have missed a short but powerful metaphor for life in modern Turkey.

Details, Details...

If you've ever taken a writing class, there's a cliché you might have heard:

Show. Don't tell.

Those three words, when fully understood, are some of the best writing advice in the whole world.*

*Also, "Don't poke your eye out with a pencil," is eight other good words of advice.

Second only to the time issue, the most common frustration I hear from students in my journaling classes is their writing in the past has felt flat and lifeless. This is usually because they are telling instead of showing. I'll give you an example.

During the summer, I guide tours in Scandinavia. On one afternoon, we take a boat ride through the Norwegian fjords. The fjords in western Norway are so spectacular, *National Geographic* once rated them the most beautiful tourist destination in the world.

People on my tours glide through this spectacular scenery, and when they journal about it, they write, "The fjords were beautiful."

Well...*duh!*

This is not a newsflash. Norway's fjords have been beautiful for thousands of years. We expect them to be beautiful before we ever see them. When we do see them, they meet that expectation. If we return home and someone asks us how the fjords were, they probably already know the fjords are beautiful. They want to know more. Writing that the fjords are "beautiful" tells very little.

Some people take this journaling mistake even further. "The fjords were *soooo* beautiful!" they write. "The fjords were the most beautiful place I have ever seen!"

If these journalers are REALLY feeling PASSIONATE about how beautiful the fjords were, they might add to the excitement with lots of CAPITAL LETTERS AND EXCLAMATION MARKS!!!!!!

They have written nothing of substance.

Don't *tell* me the fjords are beautiful. *Show* me – with lots of detail. What is it about the fjords that makes them so breathtaking? The swooping, dark granite cliffs? The sparkly clean, turquoise waters? The little maroon farmhouses that freckle the nearby land? For me, part of the fjords' beauty is the seagulls. The birds follow the boats, squawking and flapping their wings with a grace that to them is second nature. Glacier-fed waterfalls send an icy mist plunging toward rocks below. On a foggy day, the haze that settles over the water is so mystical, you expect at any moment to see a real live troll come lumbering down the mountains to grumble at you.

Details like these breathe life into your journals. If you're journaling for yourself, these details will keep your memories bright and clear long after you've returned home. If you choose to share your journals with others, people need these details in order to really feel like they were there with you.

You don't need to cover all five senses every time you write – in fact, you shouldn't. Sometimes, a particular sense might not say a lot. Just as we learned earlier about not trying to recount every single detail of your day, you also do not need to write about every sense you experience in every place you go. But take time before you write to acknowledge all of your senses. Think about them for a moment, and see if your subtler senses in any given place reveal telling details about your surroundings.

Mind Journaling

There's usually a lag between when something happens and when we get around to writing about it. Unlike photography, which allows us to capture a scene immediately and move on, most of the time when we journal, we write about our experiences hours, days, or even years after they happen. With the exception of the "verbal snapshots" we learned about in Chapter 3, most travel journaling is not "live reporting," recorded as it happens. We rely on our memories to get words onto the page.

Later on, we'll talk about long time lags – journaling after your journey is finished. But in the context of writing about your trip while it's still in progress, we still must contend with this short delay of a few hours, or a day or two, between when something happens and when we sit down to write about it. To help recall details, I use a trick I call "mind journaling."

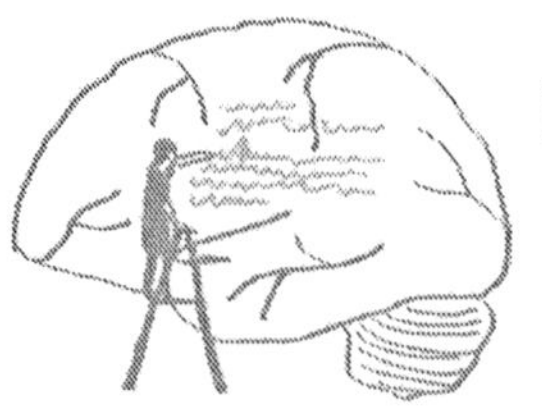

Mind journaling, as the name suggests, is simply journaling in your head – narrating journal entries in your mind as you go about your day. When you sit down to write later that day, will you remember everything you narrated in your mind? Of course not. Furthermore, you probably won't have time to write down everything you thought about. We think much faster than we write. But mind journaling helps us organize ideas ahead of time so when we do get around to writing, our thoughts flow more quickly. We've already mulled over the points we want to cover and how we want to write them.

Mind journaling is particularly useful in scanning the senses. There are things you might not notice if you don't stop to picture the scene until later. A quick scan while you are in a place will help you notice if any of your more subtle senses might be worth covering.

When we journal in our minds, we rarely think through an entire journal entry in a logical sense. We get distracted – as we should – by things around us. Multiple thoughts enter our brains simultaneously, and faced with these mental forks in the road, we meander, jumping from one topic to another in a way that would seem chaotic if we wrote them down. That's fine. We think differently from the way we write. Even though we won't recall all the words that pass through our heads, we often remember short phrases or descriptions we particularly liked. We create a mental outline to work from later.

Of course, there are times in your travels when you'll want to be fully focused on what's happening around you. Mind journaling isn't about getting so wrapped up in your head that you detach from your surroundings. When exciting things are happening that deserve your undivided attention, or when navigation or safety issues call for that same undivided attention, that's not the time to mind journal. And if you're traveling with someone else, you don't want to get so preoccupied with your mind journaling that you become anti-social. But we all have moments in our day when we're able to let part of our attention shift to what we might like to write about later.

Once you get the hang of mind journaling, you'll reach a point where you do it automatically. In moments when your mind is free to meander, you'll find it journaling on autopilot. Often, these will not be detailed journal entries, but quick observations or phrases that jump to the surface of your conscious mind for easy retrieval later. When it does come time to put your words onto paper, you'll find that key points and phrases come more quickly, enabling you to write faster, with more detail and confidence.

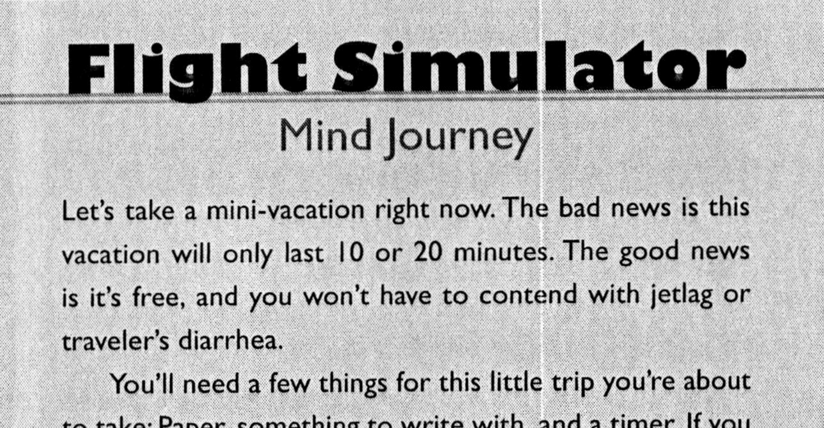

Flight Simulator

Mind Journey

Let's take a mini-vacation right now. The bad news is this vacation will only last 10 or 20 minutes. The good news is it's free, and you won't have to contend with jetlag or traveler's diarrhea.

You'll need a few things for this little trip you're about to take: Paper, something to write with, and a timer. If you don't have a timer, you can use a clock or watch – preferably something with a second hand. Get these items ready to go, but put them aside. We'll use them in Part 2 of this exercise.

Mind Journey ~ Part 1

We're going to start with a meditation exercise. If you've never meditated before, don't worry. We're not trying to levitate here. The goal is simply to quiet your mind, to minimize distractions around you so you can imagine as vividly as possible the place you have chosen to visit in this mind journey.

(If the thought of meditating really makes you squirm, you can skip the deep breathing, muscle calming parts of this exercise, close your eyes, and go. But most people find that doing the full exercise creates a nice break from the stress of their day.)

Choose a comfortable spot where you can sit. (Sitting is preferable to lying down so you don't drift off to sleep.) Now, think of a place where you've traveled in the past. It can be any place you don't currently visit on a frequent basis – a faraway country or your grandmother's house.

Begin to relax by taking a deep breath. Inhale. Exhale.

Do it again.

As you read the rest of these instructions, continue breathing in a way that's deep and comfortable. Relax your muscles as much as possible.

In a moment, you will close your eyes and keep this steady, peaceful breathing going. Once you close your eyes, sit in the darkness for a minute or two and listen to your breath. Feel your lungs fill with air and then release that air. Tune in to the rhythm of your breathing.

Once you are fully focused on your breathing, shift your attention from what your lungs are doing to how your entire body is feeling. Try to notice any tension in your body. Then, slowly, relax from head to toe.

Begin with your scalp and forehead. Visualize a warm,

soothing light. Let that light surround the top of your head in a relaxing glow that soaks the tension out of you.

When your forehead feels fully relaxed, allow the light to move slowly downward, into your facial muscles. Pay special attention to your lips and jaw. Allow them to relax naturally. If they don't want to relax right away, just keep your concentration there and keep breathing. Eventually they will loosen up.

Continue this process, scanning down your entire body. Feel the relaxing energy surround your neck and shoulders, arms and hands. Let it work its way down your chest and upper back, into to your lower back, your torso, down your thighs and calves, and finally through your ankles and into your toes.

Remember to keep breathing – deeply and slowly in a way that feels comfortable.

Once the relaxation has reached your feet, allow it to flow back up through your entire body, re-relaxing any muscles that might be trying to return to a tenser state.

Now you are ready to travel. Close your eyes and create an empty space in your mind. (But finish reading these instructions first.) Allow yourself, if only for a few minutes, to let go of any worries you might have in your life. In your empty space, imagine the place you have chosen to visit in this mind-journey. Picture it. Put yourself in that place.

Keeping your eyes closed, take a look around.

As an image forms, you can sit there for a while. Or you can start to mentally wander in the place you are picturing. You can walk, run, drive, hop a train, ride a bike — it's up to you. Allow your mind to go wherever and however it wants to go in this place you've chosen.

Keeping your eyes closed, explore for at least five minutes. If you have time, longer is even better. Stay for an hour if you like. But make it at least five minutes. (Most people don't have the patience to do this for a full hour. When you begin to feel anxious, it may be time to gently come back to reality. However, if a specific thought or memory seems to be making you anxious, try to sit with it for a moment and remind yourself you are safe now.) If you're not sure whether your five minutes are up yet, assume they're not, and linger a couple of minutes more.

When you're ready to return to the present, take a few more deep breaths. Then, open your eyes.

Come back gently. Allow yourself to sit and enjoy the relaxed feeling for a minute or two. Stretch. Yawn. When you're ready to begin writing, continue with Part 2.

Mind Journey ~ Part 2

Welcome home! Now we're going to try some speed journaling. Situate yourself someplace where you can easily see your timer or clock. Grab your paper and pen or pencil. Now, speed-journal about the five questions on the next page for two minutes each. You will probably find some of the questions easy to answer, whereas with others, your mind might go blank at first or you might think the question can't apply to the place you were in. If that happens, begin writing anyway. Write whatever comes to you. Answer the question as thoroughly as you can. And remember: Don't stop to think. Just let your words spill out of you.

When your two minutes are up for each question, finish your sentence or thought, and move on to the next question. Do this even if you feel like you have not fully answered the question you were working on. (If you find yourself in the midst of creating a masterpiece, you can always go back later and flesh things out in a less-structured timeframe. The idea here is to quickly jump from one sense to the next while the images are still fresh in your mind.)

Ready? Good. Set your timer or check the clock, and answer the following questions, spending two minutes on each.

- What did you see in the place you just visited?
- What did you hear?
- What did you taste or smell?
- How did your body feel in this place?
- How does your body feel right now?

When you're finished, read the conclusion.

Mind Journey ~ Conclusion

Most people find some senses easier to write about than others. It often depends on where you have chosen to visit. The visual sense is frequently the easiest to describe – but not always. Sense of smell or taste is sometimes trickiest. Depending on where you go, it can be the most subtle, though it can also be the most vivid.

Typically, even when people get stuck on a question or two, the overall outcome is that they can recall far more detail than they thought they could before they started the exercise.

This is a bonus to speed journaling. When we just start writing and allow our mind to go where it wants, rather than trying to direct it along any given path, when we allow ourselves to write without worrying whether our writing is "okay," details flow more naturally from our mind onto the page.

You might not be able to travel to faraway places whenever you want, but you can repeat this exercise as often as you like. It's a great way to escape for a little while. Not only is it good journaling practice, it also helps us quiet our minds and relax our bodies – something that's good for all of us.

Dave's Diaries

Yugoslavia (Now Bosnia-Herzegovina)

My most amazing, most arduous, most painfully long (and most smelly once the toilets backed up) train ride ever was a 51-hour journey from Geneva to Athens via a then-united Yugoslavia. The year was 1989. The wars that would divide the Balkans in the 1990s had not yet begun.

Traveling solo, I shared a compartment with Jamie, Jim, and John, three British travelers, all around 20 years old, like I was at the time.

We rolled through poor, rural Yugoslav villages. I had never seen anything like these places. Mesmerized, I would stand at the window of my train compartment and try to take it all in.

At one brief stop, in a village whose name I have long forgotten, I tried to photograph an elderly man on the platform. My photographic endeavor didn't work so well. Frustrated, I journaled about it at the time – about my photographic "failure." It wasn't until years later I realized my journal entry was a substitute for the picture I just wasn't meant to take.

As I wrote this entry, I began with a broad description of things around me, and then zeroed in on my photographic subject. The entry captures both a vast landscape and a specific person who unwittingly became significant in my life for a fleeting moment. It also captures a time just before the Balkan wars, when I and many other people were oblivious to the sad troubles ahead in the region.

A Train Ride Before the War

For a long time, there were no people. Just flat, lush fields of corn and sunflowers that ran clear to the skyline. The land was a fiery shade of gold, and the uninterrupted color flooded my eyes as if a sunset had left its footprint in the earth.

Then, I began to see people. I squinted to see a different brightness struggling to shine from their faces. The train twisted through remote, unexplored, tiny villages. I felt as if I had just been transported back to the 1800s.

Crumbling stucco houses with brick red rooftops splotched the countryside. There were no paved roads. Only dirt paths, carved out in occasional settlements of maybe a couple of hundred people. Chubby old women in handmade dresses rode donkey carts to move from here to there. The only other means of transportation was tractors.

In the fields, men hacked at the earth with hand tools, and girls in their late teens ushered cows around with rope leashes. Children were playing, but they had no toys. They just played with each other, and their smiles, their shrieks of excitement were as full of glee as any spoiled American child's.

These people led such different, simple lives. I could never begin to relate to them. They lacked technology. They lacked modern convenience. They also seemed to lack worry. They were sheltered from modern confusion. I wondered if they were happier than me.

A train passing through town was their day's entertainment, and they would all come out to wave to the Westerners who gawked back at them. They watched us as our train twisted slowly through their villages, their faces ablaze with curiosity. We were strangers from faraway lives passing through their insignificant scrap of planet. Strangers like me came every day, foreign creatures who never stopped to say hello.

All I could do was stand at the window and watch this neglected culture flit by. Like a program on public television, life outside seemed very far away. Snatches of lives kept racing past. I had about seven seconds to take in each one.

We rumbled through some more realistic sized towns.

Not cities by any means, but there was some sense of organization. There were paved roads with names. There were automobiles. The buildings were of stucco, dirtied by the polluted air. Laundry hung from the windows.

We stopped about once an hour at a train station in one of these villages. The benches in the stations seemed the fashionable place to be. Men sat, one leg crossed over the opposite knee, the way southern European men often sit, lazily smoking cigarettes. A group of four young girls trying to catch a glimpse of the people on the train giggled in embarrassment when I turned around to find them watching me reload my camera.

An old man crouched against a lamppost, and for a few minutes of his life, I studied him through the window, secretly reading the story in his eyes. He wore a blue and white embroidered skullcap. His yellowish skin was wrinkled. A carefully tailored beard ornamented his face. He was alone, dragging long on a cigarette. He had lived hard and simple, and it showed in the trenches of his skin.

I had to have a picture of him.

I snapped on my zoom lens and waited until he turned away. I didn't want him to notice me. I focused, then lowered my camera. I was waiting until just the right moment when he would be looking off to the side so I could shoot. Just the right pose, with the smoldering stick of tobacco braced between his tense lips. I was afraid he might get up and leave. I was afraid the train might pull out of the station.

And then – *CLICK* – I got him.

"Hey," I whispered, pulling John over to the window. "See that guy over there?"

"Yeah."

"I just got an amazing picture of him."

The train pulled away.

"Oh, NO!"

"What's wrong?" John asked.

"I just changed my film. My camera was set at the wrong speed. It was overexposed."

It was such an easy error to make. It was too late to be corrected. The man was gone forever.

Dave's Diaries

Somewhere in the Pacific Ocean

In Chapter 6, we'll explore the ways the outer journey sets the stage for our inner journey. Specifically, when we're in unfamiliar cultures, hidden aspects of our personality can emerge – lured to the surface of our mind by either the unfamiliarities around us, or by our distance from our own familiarities. Sometimes, however, as the following journal entry shows, the landscape alone (or in this case, the seascape) can be enough to offer powerful insights into ourselves.

This next excerpt is from the same trip through the South Pacific I mentioned earlier. It was my first time in that part of the world, and my first time so far out in the ocean, so far from land.

I've always been a night person. I love being awake and alone, late at night, when I know nobody will bother me. At home, I can sit in front of my fireplace for hours and let the flames hypnotize me. At sea, I found a different late-night ritual, which gave me a new perspective on the space I occupy on our giant planet.

Perspective

I've found a new night routine on this ship. Late at night, maybe one a.m., after the restaurants and bars have all closed and all the other passengers have gone to bed, I walk outside and stare out at the blackness.

My stateroom is on deck three. Deck three is also the level of the ship where the deck wraps all the way around the ship. In daytime, the deck always has motion – other passengers doing laps around the ship. Three-and-a-half laps equal a mile. But late at night, deck three is my private deck. The ocean is my private ocean.

The ship plows through the water, throwing waves to the sides. The water never stops moving. Never. The sound of the ship's waves is constant, yet constantly changing.

Each slice of time, each millisecond, has its own shape in the water.

The Pacific Ocean is littered with thousands of ships, yet I could circle deck three until sunrise, and probably never see a single one of them. That's how huge this ocean is.

My vision extends maybe 20 feet into the blackness. There is no end point, no defined place where it all stops. I stare into nothing. I can't tell what's out there. I can't see where the sea and horizon meet. I feel incredibly small.

As we sail closer to the equator, the humidity is growing heavier, like a warm, wet blanket that weighs me down.

At 1:30 a.m., I hear a voice behind me. It's Seth, an American who lives in Tokyo. Like me, Seth's brother is a guest lecturer on the ship. Seth has been up in an abandoned bar, at the only time when he could practice the piano there.

I tell him what I've been thinking about – about the smallness.

"This entire ship," he says, "is just a speck in the ocean."

He is right. And I am just a microspeck.

CHAPTER 5

Eluding Your Inner Censor

Are you enjoying yourself so far? I am! I am currently on a tropical island, enjoying a late afternoon snack of champagne and lobster, and basking in my millions of dollars in book royalties.

Oh, wait. No. That's Stephen King.

Very well then. Let's continue.

Before we delve into the inner journey, we're going to spend the next two chapters exploring the psychology of journaling and the psychology of travel. With a better understanding of these two things, you'll write more freely about your inner journey. You'll gain deeper insights from your travels, and because you've journaled about those insights, you'll retain them long after your journeys are finished. We'll start with the psychology of journaling. It's time to go stare down an annoying little creature who lives in your brain: Your Inner Censor.*

Nearly all writers have an Inner Censor patrolling their thoughts. Some Inner Censors are more vocal than others. Often, we can't hear them, but we feel their presence;

*Don't worry. I've got your back. Nobody's going to get hurt.

we sense their uptight attempts to shut us up. If you've ever sat down to write, and suddenly heard a faint but insistent voice saying, "No! You can't write that," that's your Inner Censor talking.

Don't write that because it's not good writing. Don't write that because somebody might not like it. Don't write that because it's not polite. Don't write that because it's embarrassing. Don't write that because somebody might read it. Don't write that because no one will want to read it. Don't write that because it's a lie. Don't write that because it's the truth. Don't write that because maybe it's true and maybe it isn't, but writing it might make it feel true. Don't write that because if you write it, your words might leap off the page like an angry raccoon and sink their painfully sharp (albeit kind of cute) teeth into you and give you rabies.

Yowch!

But our words can't really do that. They're just words. Our Inner Censors need to chill out.

Writing about ourselves can be nerve wracking. We fear our words aren't good enough, or they're too revealing, or they go against some "rule" we've been taught about how we should think. Inner Censors love to stir up this fear. Their job is to regulate what we write in an attempt to shield us from our own thoughts. Inner Censors aren't concerned with good writing. They mean well, but they're overzealous, like overprotective parents who won't let us go out and play because something bad might happen. Ultimately, they can hold us back from writing what we really want to write. Most Inner Censors are way too sensitive. They tell us not to write down all sorts of things that could potentially make for more exciting journals or big discoveries about ourselves.

Once you get to know your Inner Censor, and discover his or her *modus operandi*, you'll be able to make more conscious decisions about your writing instead of letting your Inner Censor make those decisions for you. When you do this, you'll find your journals become more alive – more "you."

Exploring the Iceberg

Imagine for a moment that your mind is an iceberg.* Ten percent is above water. The other 90 percent is submerged. The 10 percent above water is your conscious mind. The submerged 90 percent consists of things you are not thinking about right now.

*And what a witty and intelligent iceberg it is!

Your Inner Censor's job is to patrol the waters around the submerged part of the iceberg, snorkel in hand, ready to dive down and drag you back to the water's surface if you try to jump in. He doesn't want you to go beneath the water level for fear that you might drown. But unlike swimming around a real iceberg, it's safe to dive deep into your mind. Sometimes it's scary, but your thoughts are merely thoughts. They're not going to drown you. On the contrary, going for a dive and exploring what's down there gives you a new perspective on yourself. Especially while traveling, away from your everyday routines, you might discover things you like about yourself that you didn't know were there.

The exposed part of your mental iceberg contains everything you're aware of at this moment. As you sit and read this book, you might be picturing an iceberg, or your Inner Censor swimming around the periphery. You might be aware of the place you are reading this, or the way your body feels, or distractions around you.

Just below the surface, in the shallow depths of your subconscious, are mundane things you can quickly bring to the surface without effort. You probably weren't thinking about what you ate for breakfast when you started reading this chapter.* Breakfast was below the level of your immediate awareness. But now

*Unless you're eating it right now

that I've mentioned it, this thought might have risen to the surface. You have millions of other benign thoughts swimming in your mind such as what you did last weekend, upcoming appointments, or friends' birthdays. These thoughts are okay with your Inner Censor. He'll let them come to the surface. Deeper beneath the surface, your Inner Censor gets more selective about what he's willing to let come up for air.

Our Inner Censors go into overdrive when we journal because journaling is a genre of writing where we root around in our thoughts a lot. Our Inner Censors work extra, extra hard when we travel because in unfamiliar places, we often encounter thoughts that are very different from our everyday experiences. We might uncover fears or frustrations, confusion or feelings of inadequacy, the crankiness that is born out of travel fatigue, or judgments and prejudices about unfamiliar cultures that we don't want to have, but which are inevitable on some level when we stray from familiarity. Our Inner Censor does what he or she can to limit these thoughts. But when we keep uncomfortable thoughts down in our subconscious, rather than untangling them and checking them out, the thoughts tend to stay trapped inside our heads, and they surface in ways we're not even aware of.

Woof!

I'll give you an example. When I was six, I was knocked down and terrorized by a neighborhood puppy. He gobbled up the lower part of my jacket, but fortunately left only a few surface scratches on my body. I wasn't seriously hurt, but the incident terrified me. To make matters worse, the neighbor kids who owned the dog watched and laughed as I went home crying.

Two decades later, shortly after I moved to Seattle, I started dating someone who was the doting parent of a Golden Retriever. My girlfriend, Megan, couldn't understand why I got so nervous around Chakra, but every time the dog came near me, I tensed all of my muscles.

"What's the problem?" Megan asked me one day. "Were you attacked by a dog as a child or something?"

She asked her question in a sarcastic tone. She was annoyed I didn't love Chakra as much as she did. I don't think she expected me to say yes.

And the crazy thing is: my first answer was no. No, I was never attacked by a dog as a child. But I stopped myself in mid-thought, and all of a sudden, I could picture my six-year-old self, two houses down the hill from the house where I grew up, on my back in the grass, screaming in terror, pleading with this playful puppy to get off of me. The memory was intense. I could remember the blue baseball jacket I had been wearing, scraps of it vanishing into Tuffy's mouth. I could remember the dry grass against my skin, and the upside-down perspective of my neighbor's house as I lay on my back, tormented by this overexcited ball of fur who was barking all over me and nipping with his teeth.

Because the "attack" by Tuffy, the neighbor dog, hadn't left any physical scars, I had forgotten the incident long ago. I hadn't wiped it from my mind altogether, however. My Inner Censor was letting me recall it in a subconscious, limited context. My Inner Censor would only let parts of the memory surface – the parts that told me dogs were dangerous. That message would reverberate every time I saw a dog, even though the specific incident that had led me to that belief was floating much deeper in my subconscious where I couldn't easily retrieve it. Recalling it, however, was exactly what I needed to do. It gave me an adult perspective on a childhood trauma. Tuffy had never hurt me physically, nor had he intended to.

A month after she asked me the question, Megan was stunned one day to walk into her living room and find me wrestling playfully with Chakra, a dog three times the size of Tuffy. The dog

I had been so jumpy around weeks before was now barking up a storm at me, and I was barking back. Chakra was gnawing on my arm. I was flipping Chakra on her back and then letting her pounce on top of me. The dog and I were both having a good laugh.

For years, my Inner Censor had stopped me from recalling my childhood dog memory. Once Megan helped drag it to the surface, I realized my fear of dogs for so many years had been irrational. Once I got past my Inner Censor, Chakra and I became pals.

This story has nothing to do with traveling or journaling, but it illustrates a point to keep in mind when you write: There are many thoughts in our minds that our Inner Censors try to keep so far below the surface that we can't dive down and see them. But with practice, we can learn to swim around safely in our subconscious minds and discover fascinating things about ourselves. This is especially powerful when traveling because the world around us has changed from our usual environment, and it nudges our thoughts in new directions.

Dive Fast!

How do you get past your Inner Censor so you can really explore the depths of your mind? It's easier than you might think.

Inner Censors don't like change. One of your Inner Censor's main goals is to maintain your status quo, and keep you as you have always been. His or her resistance to change is what makes it relatively easy to sneak past. You are used to operating in a certain way, and your Inner Censor is used to you operating in that way. If you catch your Inner Censor off guard, you can fake him out and blow past before he knows what happened.

This is another way Speed Journaling is so productive. In addition to the simple matter of time, and getting a lot written in a limited number of minutes, when you Speed Journal, you write faster than your Inner Censor can keep up with. He or she is used to you stopping and turning around when he or she tells you to stop and turn around. So go fast. Fake your Inner Censor out. When your Inner Censor orders you to halt, tell him or her, "No!"*

*And stick out your tongue as you speed by!

Flight Simulator

Retire Your Inner Censor ~ Part 1

My Inner Censor is a nervous little guy with frazzled hair and panicky wide eyes. He keeps his arms spread apart like a soccer goalie, trying to stop certain thoughts from getting past.

What does your Inner Censor look like? Is it male or female? (It doesn't have to be the same sex as you!) How big is your Inner Censor? What is its personality like? How about its voice? Does he or she talk fast or slow? Loud or soft? What sorts of mannerisms does your Inner Censor have? How about an accent? Does he or she have a name?

For this exercise, find a sheet of paper separate from your journal. It's okay to use a sheet of paper from your journal, but if you do, tear it out before you do anything else with it. Find a place to write where you will not leave an indentation on anything below.

Now, draw a picture of your Inner Censor. Even if you think you are the world's lousiest artist, draw your Inner Censor anyway. You can use a pen or pencil, magic markers, crayons, even watercolors. Whatever you do, use a regular-sized sheet of paper – nothing fancy. You'll see why shortly.

When you're finished drawing, move on to Part 2.

Retire Your Inner Censor ~ Part 2

Your Inner Censor has been with you for a long time now – probably as long as you can remember. All these years, he or she has been working hard to protect you from your thoughts. A little too hard. Your Inner Censor is getting in your way.

Write a letter to your Inner Censor. Explain why you need to go against his or her wishes. Explain why it's time for him or her to retire.

As you write your letter, keep in mind that although your Inner Censor might seem irritating or in the way at times, he means well. He has struggled all these years to "protect" you. It's just that he's not efficient.

If you're angry at your Inner Censor, it's okay to express that. If you want to thank your Inner Censor for his hard work, that's great too. Maybe you feel sad that it's time for him to go. Or maybe even a little frightened. He's been a big part of you all these years. Whatever you feel a need to express or explain, be honest. Don't let your Inner Censor censor your letter!

Whatever tone you take, conclude your letter firmly. Explain to your Inner Censor that it's time for him or her to go.

When you're finished writing your letter, move on to Part 3 of this exercise.

Retire Your Inner Censor ~ Part 3

Your Inner Censor should be sitting right next to you in the picture you've created. You have just officially retired him. Now it's time for your Inner Censor to go have fun – far away from his job of guarding your thoughts. He's been in the way but he has worked hard. He deserves a reward for his efforts – in a place where he won't bother you.

Think for a moment about where you'd like to send your Inner Censor. It should be a place you don't intend to visit yourself so you don't bump into him later. If you're keeping your own travel options open, keep in mind that your Inner Censor does not have a physical body, and is therefore immune to the risks we mortals face when we travel. Given the amount of corruption and crime, I personally wouldn't hang out on the beach in Nigeria, but my Inner Censor will be just fine there. He'll enjoy the sun and the sea.

Now – and I really mean this – send your Inner Censor to whatever place you have chosen. Find the address of a nice hotel, or a cruise ship company, or a tour operator located in the faraway place where you are sending your Inner Censor. An easy way to do this is to look up your destination on the Internet. With a quick search on the destination's name, and the word, "tourism," you can find a lovely hotel or some other place for your Inner Censor to spend retirement.

Address an envelope to that place. Be sure to put enough international postage on the envelope. Take the picture you drew of your Inner Censor and seal him or her inside the envelope. DO NOT put a return address on the envelope!

Take your Inner Censor to a mailbox and send him on his way.

Once your Inner Censor is gone, he might send you mental postcards from time to time, and these postcards will often be in the same nagging tone he has always used with you. From now on, when you hear his voice telling you not to write something, when you feel him breathing down your neck, shielding you from your true thoughts, remind him nicely but firmly that he no longer lives in your brain. He now lives in Nigeria, or China, Jamaica, Timbuktu, or wherever you have sent him. He needs to stay there now. You'll get along just fine without him!

Some people love the above exercise. Others think it's ridiculous. If you skipped over it, even if you do think it's ridiculous, I encourage you to try it when you have time. There is something about the ritual of saying goodbye to our Inner Censors, of thanking them for their efforts and sending them on their way, that really can tell our mind on a subconscious level that it's okay to write deeper than we have written in the past.

Write Like Nobody's Looking!

When I was younger, I hated dancing. Absolutely hated it – not because I didn't think it was fun, but because I was thoroughly convinced I danced with the finesse of an ostrich. I was certain, every time I was dragged onto a dance floor, that everybody else in the room was staring at me, silently cackling about the awkward, short kid who appeared to be having a seizure.

The fact is, I probably *did* look like I was having a seizure – not because I lacked coordination, but because I was so petrified about what everyone else was thinking that I couldn't relax. Then one day, I read a line in one of those self-help books that are one part great advice, eight parts sappy drivel, and this one line stuck with me: "Dance like nobody's looking."

I embraced that idea. I learned to relax. Now when I dance, I have no clue whether I'm any good or not. Maybe I really do look like an ostrich. Maybe everyone *is* staring at me. But I don't care; therefore, I have fun.

The same concept works with writing.

"What if somebody finds my journal and reads it?" That is probably the most common phobia among journalers of all sorts. What if I pour my deepest, darkest travel secrets into the pages of my notebook, confess all of my weaknesses, my confusions, every single wrong turn I take, and then somebody reads it all? What if someone finds my journal in its secret hiding place after I get home? What if I lose it somewhere on my trip and the editor of a sleazy British tabloid finds it and publishes it, verbatim – not just my personal confessions, but all of my spelling and punctuation errors as well? What if, on the way home, my plane goes down in a fiery crash, there are no survivors, and the *only* thing that gets salvaged from the smoldering wreckage is my extremely private travel diary, still in pristine, legible condition, exposing every private thought I have ever had?"

Sounds irrational? It is. That's what phobias are – irrational fears, but fears that *feel* very real. The fear of someone reading your journal when you don't want them to can stifle your best writing.

Let's take a moment to confront this phobia of prying eyes. If you write like nobody's looking, you will write more honest prose that fully captures the spirit of your travels.

How can you be absolutely, 100 percent certain that unwanted eyes will never stumble across your pages? You can't. You also cannot be absolutely, 100 percent certain that the proverbial bus won't run you over in the next 24 hours, but if you are a reasonably intelligent human, you can take basic precautions to minimize the risk of both of the aforementioned catastrophes.

As far as the bus goes, look both ways, and ignore the neighborhood bully who told you to go play in traffic. When it comes to your journal, if you don't want others to read it, do what you can to keep it with you when traveling. Carry it in your day bag, or stash it at the bottom of your backpack or suitcase. When you're home, if you have family or roommates of any sort who are inclined to snoop, find a good hiding spot. Seal your journal in a large envelope if you don't plan to read it for a while, buy yourself a cheap safe to lock it in, or if you must, adopt a pit bull to guard it. Take whatever precautions will make you feel comfortable. Then, don't worry about it. Whatever you need to do for some peace of mind, figure out a plan *before* you begin traveling, so that when you're on the road, you don't have the fear of discovery tiptoeing around in your brain.

With the more farfetched scenarios – what if a stranger finds it, or what if you suddenly die from tainted airline food* – I find that a fatalistic approach puts my mind at ease. What if I unexpectedly bite the dust? I won't be around to face the fallout from anything I've written, so why worry? What if I lose my journal along the way and a stranger finds it? *Hmmph.* Jerry Springer is syndicated internationally these days. My own scandalous thoughts are boring in comparison. (One thing I do, in case I ever do leave my journal somewhere while traveling is write my e-mail address in large letters inside the front cover. I can stop at any Internet café to see if anyone is trying to return it to me.)

*A much more likely cause of death than a dramatic crash, if you ask me

Again, there is no 100 percent guarantee that your journal will never be viewed by unwelcome eyes. Look for an air-tight solution and you'll drive yourself crazy. But be realistic about the likelihood, and do what you can to let go of your fear. Write like nobody's looking and your words will dance across your pages more freely.

Owning Your Words

Censoring one's own thoughts is a common affliction among writers. When we write for others to read – something we'll discuss in Chapter 9 – *that's* when it's appropriate to start reeling in some of your words and thoughts, and editing them for public consumption. But when you write your initial journal entries, write for yourself and write boldly. And remember, saying goodbye to your Inner Censor doesn't mean you must write down every single thought that flits through your mind. In the middle of a vacation, there may be issues you don't feel like writing about, and that's fine. What's important is that *you* make that call. Your Inner Censor doesn't decide for you.

Dave's Diaries

Shikhov, Azerbaijan (Well...sort of.)

For me, writing a letter to my Inner Censor and firing him was the easy part. It took me about 20 minutes. I made my point and bade him farewell. The hard part was figuring out where to send him. It needed to be someplace in the world I will never travel – but I want to travel everywhere.

I pondered a few places that are unsafe. But places change, and sometimes unsafe places become safe. I pondered places I am currently not allowed to visit, such as North Korea. But hey, that could change too one day; besides, if sent from America to North Korea, my Inner Censor would probably just get intercepted at the post office, scrutinized by someone charged with keeping America safe, and then either tossed in the trash, or stuffed in a file for further scrutiny if world events warranted it. I suppose that would be fine since I will never get anywhere near that file myself, but I really wanted to send my Inner Censor far – not just to some boring government office in Washington, DC.

Suddenly, Azerbaijan popped into my mind. I'm not sure why; I guess it just seemed like a remote place. "But I want to go there too," I thought.

Nevertheless, I hopped online and Googled "Azerbaijan beach." Maybe there was someplace in the country I could avoid if I ever do get to go there.

Up on my screen popped Shikhov Beach. A click over to Wikipedia offered this description: "...The water is polluted by sewage and industrial waste and the view is marred by large oil rigs both in the surrounding land area and offshore."

Perfect! I would never go to such a beach. My Inner Censor, on the other hand, will be just fine there.

Another minute of searching led me to a hotel just down the

road from the beach. For the cost of an international postage stamp, I sent my Inner Censor to his retirement home – far, far away – to splash and play in waters where I will never swim.

All I needed to do now was break the bittersweet news to my Inner Censor that our time together was finished. Here's what I wrote:

A Letter to My Inner Censor

Dear Inner Censor,

Listen, dude, breaking up is always tough, but it's time for you to go. I mean, seriously, I never actually invited you into my brain in the first place. You just kind of showed up one day.

I'm not sure when you showed up. During high school, perhaps, when I started to take writing seriously? Yeah, that's probably it. I remember one day when you ran amok in my poetry.

You know that book I used to write in? I called it my "Escape Book," for the sole reason that on its cover was a fragment of a free bumper sticker I had picked up at a rest stop – somewhere in...Wisconsin, I think. "Escape to Wisconsin," the sticker said. Or maybe it was "Escape to Wyoming" or "Escape to New Jersey." I don't remember, but I cut out that one word, "Escape," and plastered it diagonally across the cover of my poetry notebook.

There's this one poem I wrote in that notebook one day – a not particularly good poem, if I recall. Come to think of it, I'm not sure it was even a poem. I think it was just a string of sappy, nostalgic, random memories of my childhood in London that I wrote the night before I was about to fly back there for the first time in eight years.

So...I wrote the thing, and then a few weeks later, after my trip was over, I crossed it all out with a thick black magic marker so neither I, nor anyone else, could ever read it again.

And the thing is, Inner Censor, that's the most screamingly blatant example I can find of your work. The real messes you've made are less tangible. The real havoc you have wrought on my writing lies in the things I never wrote at all, because you've been hanging out in my brain, stashing them away in some hidden "no-write zone" where I can't get to them.

You don't seriously think that's helping me, do you? Do you think if I don't write stuff down, it doesn't exist? It's still stuck somewhere in my mind, and you know it. It's in there, and it could become my best writing if I could get it out. Or it could be some of my worst writing, but maybe I'd learn things from it that I need to learn.

Inner Censor, I know you've meant well, but I've been thinking about all of your good intentions, and I'm sorry to say this, but they're irrelevant. They're dragging down my creativity. They're preventing me from writing what I really want to write. And you know what, I.C.? It's *my* writing. Not yours. Mine mine mine! You need to leave it alone.

So listen, I've been thinking, and I've decided it's time for us to part company. Permanently. You need to go.

Don't worry. I'm going to send you someplace where you can relax. You can retire and lounge on the beach all day. The weather's nice there, and you'll never have to work again. Seriously! Think about it; for the rest of your life, you can just chill out and do nothing. Or if you get restless, if you really must go back to censoring someone's thoughts, maybe you can find a corrupt politician or something – someone who needs more censoring than I do.

But you need to go, I.C. – out of my brain! Sorry buddy, but I've got writing to do, and I just can't work with all of your distractions.

Love,
Dave

CHAPTER 6

The Joy of Culture Shock

Whenever we leave our familiar lives and travel to places where things are different, a big message rattles our thoughts:

"Toto, I don't think we're in Kansas anymore."

Arriving in unfamiliar territory is like that scene in *The Wizard of Oz* when Dorothy first opens her eyes after the twister. She's surrounded by people who look and talk, think and behave differently from herself. She doesn't know where to go or what to do. She relies on the local inhabitants to lead her down the Yellow Brick Road. She's nervous. She's lost. She embarks on a journey that ultimately gives her a new understanding of herself and her life at home. But to get that understanding, she must go to where she is the outsider, where talking lions, tin men, witches, and munchkins are the normal ones.*

*And you thought Azerbaijan sounded exotic.

The Wizard of Oz is the perfect metaphor for culture shock, and for the personal insights we gain traveling in unfamiliar places. Just as Dorothy learns so much about herself on her journey, so can we, away from our familiar cultures. But it's easy to lose those insights when we return to our everyday lives. Journaling about them as we travel, we have a way to bundle them up and take them home so we don't forget them.*

*Dorothy didn't have to keep a travel journal. She had Hollywood film producers to document her journey. Most of us don't have that luxury.

In this chapter, we'll look at the unique psychology that comes with being in unfamiliar surroundings. What does this have to do with travel journaling? It's what makes travel journaling different from, and in some ways more powerful than, journaling at home. When we change our surroundings, those surroundings change us. Understanding the ways we shift our realities in foreign places helps us write about our inner journeys more fully.

We're going to define "foreign" in a new way in this chapter. I'll show you how you can go be foreign in your own neighborhood. If that's not enough to entice you, I will also give you an excuse to go take a road trip for a day when you think you should stay home and do laundry.

Your Cultural Comfort Zones

Think for a moment about the places in the world where you're most comfortable, places where you feel completely yourself. They could be places close by – your home, your job or school, a local park, a favorite coffee shop or restaurant, or the darkness of a theater. Or they might be familiar but faraway places, like the neighborhood where you grew up, a relative's house, or a place where you spend frequent vacations.

Now think for a moment about the people you're most comfortable with. Are they your family? Friends? A significant other? Co-workers? People in a particular group you belong to? What is it about these people or places that puts you at ease? How long have you known these people or places?

We all have places where we feel safe, places where we can

"be ourselves" – or where if we can't be ourselves, we at least know what's expected of us. These places feel familiar. We know the "rules" there. Usually these rules aren't written, and often, they've never been explained to us. We might not even think of these rules as rules. They might not seem restrictive. They're just how we live. They guide us. Often, we like the rules in our lives. They are, we believe, the way things should be.

Now think for a moment about times in your life when you've felt uncomfortable. Do you remember your first day of school? I do. I still remember what my kindergarten classroom looked like. It had a low sink with a water fountain spigot. I remember the water fountain because on the first day, not sure what else to do with myself, I kept getting drinks of water.* We had all met our teacher, said our names, and sung the "Wheels on the Bus" song. Now it was time to socialize. Time to hang out and explore, get to know our classmates, work the room, and look for lucrative networking opportunities. But I didn't know anyone and I was shy. So I'd find an activity and amuse myself for the few minutes my five-year-old attention span could handle. Then I'd realize I was in a room full of people I didn't know and I'd try to look busy. At age five, getting a drink of water seemed like the extremely important, busy thing to do. I felt excited to be at my first day of school, but I also felt a bit confused. I didn't know what I was doing. I just had to wing it.

*I also remember the bathroom quite well.

As adults, we experience these awkward times too. We go to parties where we don't know people. We join clubs or start new jobs. We decide to get in better shape and join a gym, but we walk into that gym for the first time feeling out of shape compared to the regulars, not knowing how the equipment works, convinced that the second we start working out, all other activity in the room will stop as everyone turns to stare at the flabby newcomer who's lifting the scrawny-person weights.*

*Okay, maybe I'm projecting here.

Traveling isn't so different. When we go to unfamiliar places, we find ourselves surrounded by people different from us. They might speak a different language or dialect, use different body language, dress differently, or have a different sense of personal space or appropriate speaking volume. They might have political or religious views we disagree with or have never encountered. They might have different interests, different ways to entertain themselves, different senses of what's funny and what isn't. They might eat differently, drink differently, or be more open or more guarded than we are about discussing personal issues such as health, money, or sex. When we encounter these situations, we've entered a foreign environment. Not necessarily a foreign country, but an environment that's foreign to us, in which we are outsiders.

The farther from home we stray geographically, the farther we tend to get from our own set of subcultures. Away from the people we interact with on a regular basis, we step away from their expectations of us – and, more importantly, we step away from our expectations of their expectations. Getting away from our familiar lives frees us to try on different shades of our personalities that we might not try on at home, and see how we like them.

This can lead to big personal discoveries. Often, however, these potential discoveries tiptoe quietly around the fringes of our conscious minds. As we journal about the foreign environment around us, and how that environment is affecting our thoughts and behaviors, we become more aware of these emerging pieces of who we are. Writing them down helps solidify them, so we don't just revert back to our old selves when we return home.

Our Multicultural Selves

We each know how to operate within dozens of different subcultures. When I'm traveling abroad and someone asks where I'm from, my first answer is usually the United States. If I want to be more specific, I might say Seattle. But "American" barely scratches the surface of my cultural identity. I have ancestry from Norway, Germany, Poland, and Russia. I was raised by a Lutheran mother and a Jewish father who took me to a Unitarian church on Sundays. Now I follow Taoism, a Chinese philosophy. I was born in California. I've lived in England, Norway, Turkey, Maryland, Wisconsin, and Washington state. All of those things are *part* of my list of personal subcultures. In addition, we have other subcultures not tied to geography, ethnicity, or religion.

I'm a writer. I'm a tour guide. I've worked with deaf people. I've done extreme low-budget travel, and worked on luxury cruise ships. I was born in the late 1960s. I went to high school in the 1980s. I play the fiddle. I'm short. I've taught English to refugees. I like well-crafted Belgian beers and scruffy dive bars. I listen to baroque music, Celtic folk, and old-school punk. I've never been married or had kids. I'm male. I blog. I own a car. Sometimes I take the bus. I own a condominium.*

*Okay, technically, my bank still owns my condo, but that's beside the point.

Each of these details has a subculture linked to it – a group of people or an environment in which I operate with some level of comfort and familiarity. Within each of our subcultures, we learn a set of "rules" as to which behaviors are appropriate. I behave one way around friends, another when I work with freelance clients, another when I guide tours, another when I'm with family. I follow one set of rules at rock concerts, a very different set at symphonies. At a rock concert in a big arena, it might be culturally acceptable to stand up and scream. (And, if it happens to be an aging, bad hair band from the 1980s, it's acceptable to wave a cigarette lighter in the air.*) But if I behaved that way at a symphony, I would get whacked over the head with a tuba and asked to leave. On the other hand,

*WOOOO!!! Free Bird!!!!

if I went to a punk show and sat quietly in my chair, clapping politely after each song and whispering to the people around me about how dramatic that final crescendo sounded, I would not get kicked out. I would get kicked. Hard. I know how to act at a fancy restaurant versus a blue collar dive bar, at a football game versus a grocery store,* and so on. Every industry, every hobby, every generation, every situation we find ourselves in, has its own set of behaviors that the people within these groups follow.

*Please don't punt the melons!

When we travel to a foreign place, our understanding of local behaviors isn't so clear. The way we eat, the way we dress, the way we talk, walk, pay for something, make a phone call, greet a stranger, greet a friend, order in a restaurant, catch a taxi, blow our nose, use the toilet, bathe, drive, flirt, compliment someone, accept a compliment, all vary from culture to culture. When we find ourselves in a culture where we're outsiders, we might not know how these things are done. We have to wing it – just like I did on my first day of kindergarten, just like Dorothy did when she landed in Oz.

Our comfort zones are defined by the cultures in which we know how to operate. Each of us has a set of personal cultures, based on a wide array of factors:

- Where we live
- Where we have lived before
- Language(s)
- Accents or dialects
- Race
- Religion
- Gender
- Sexual orientation
- Education
- Career
- Body size
- Family size and structure

- Marital or relationship status
- Whether or not we have or want children
- Age
- Income level
- Political views or affiliations
- Medical conditions
- Clubs, hobbies, sports, or other activities we participate in

These are just a few of them.

Flight Simulator

What Are Your Subcultures?

Using the preceding list of defining elements as a guide, make a list of your different subcultures.

After you make your list, ask yourself the following questions:

- How many of your subcultures are cultures you were born into?
- How many are cultures you have adopted or stumbled upon later in life?
- Which ones are your core cultures – those you feel fully connected with – and which ones are cultures you understand to an extent, but are not fully immersed in?

Now, make a list of at least ten subcultures that do not make up a part of who you are. Among your list of subcultures that you don't feel you belong in or understand, are there any you would like to experience? What could you do to make that happen? Are there others you choose to avoid? If so, why?

Sometimes, when we start paying attention to *all* of the different subcultures in which we operate, we discover surprises. I began working as a tour guide in my mid-20s. On one of my very first tours, I worked as an assistant guide in Italy. All of the people in my tour group were American. All of them were significantly older than me.

One night in Siena, I took shelter from a pounding rainstorm in a local bar with three people from my group. One of the tour members was sipping a cup of coffee when she looked down the bar at two college students. The students were both drinking bright-red cocktails made with Campari.

"Oh, look at those red drinks," the woman from my group said, assuming the students didn't understand English. "Don't they look delicious?"

But the students spoke English well. "It's the best drink in Italy," one of them smiled. "You must try one."

"I don't drink," said the woman from my group. "But I bet Dave will try one."

I felt like Mikey from those Life cereal commercials in the 1970s and '80s. But the drink looked more enticing than a bowl of cereal,* so I made the extreme cultural sacrifice and ordered a drink. I began chatting with the two students.

The next thing I knew, an hour had passed, and somewhere along the line, my three tour members had left without me. I stayed and chatted with Massimo and Paolo, my two new Italian friends, until the bar

*Why are people so into cereal? You take something crunchy and douse it in milk, which makes it soggy. Then you have to put sugar on it to make it edible. Could I have some leftover cold pizza instead, please?

finally closed. As I walked back to my hotel, I felt fulfilled in a way I hadn't felt in weeks.

Within America, each generation has its own culture. I had been away from 20-something culture for a long time. Being around people my own age again, I reconnected with one of my subcultures. Even though Massimo and Paolo were from a country that was foreign to me, we connected culturally in ways I had not connected with people in my tour groups – people from my own country – because of our age difference.

So the concept of "culture" isn't as straightforward as we might think. We have cultures in which we belong, cultures in which we don't belong, and cultures in which we might not fully belong, but which we have some understanding of.

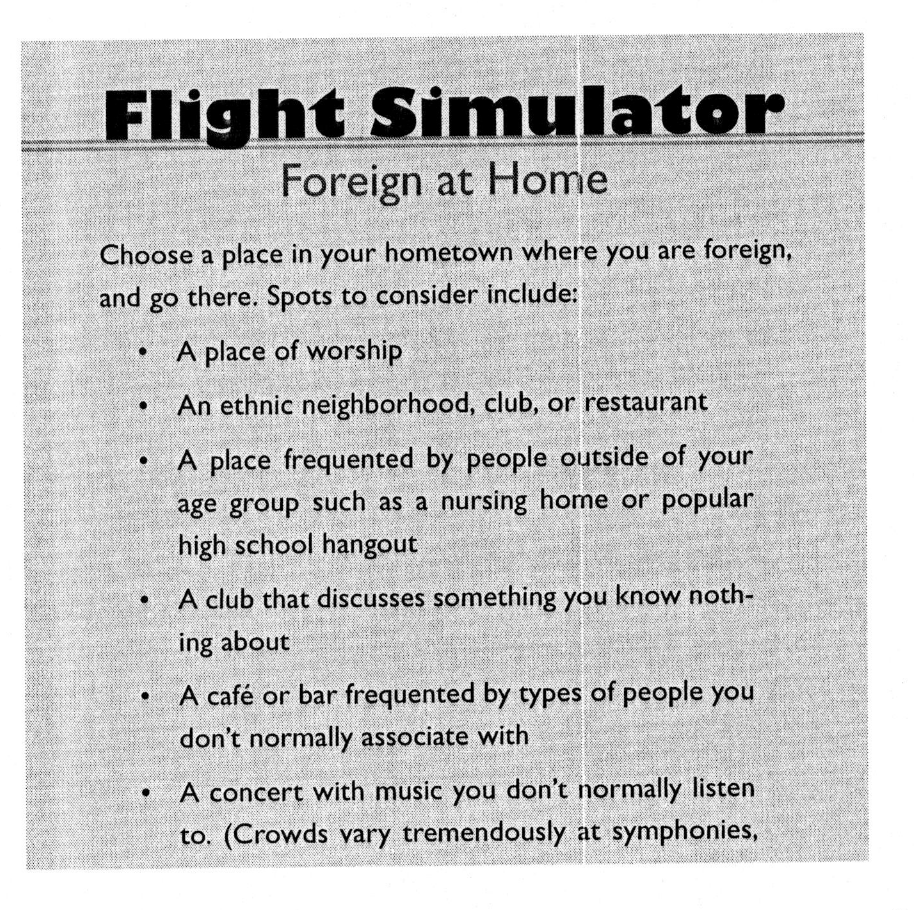

Flight Simulator

Foreign at Home

Choose a place in your hometown where you are foreign, and go there. Spots to consider include:

- A place of worship
- An ethnic neighborhood, club, or restaurant
- A place frequented by people outside of your age group such as a nursing home or popular high school hangout
- A club that discusses something you know nothing about
- A café or bar frequented by types of people you don't normally associate with
- A concert with music you don't normally listen to. (Crowds vary tremendously at symphonies,

punk shows, country-western concerts, and Zydeco dances.)

- A meeting for a political group you don't affiliate with

There are hundreds of other possibilities. Get creative.

If you're worried about feeling awkward or out of place at the spot you have chosen, you've made a good choice. The idea in this exercise is to step out of your comfort zone and get as foreign as possible. It's natural to feel worried that you'll stand out. Take a deep breath and go anyway.

Before you go, journal about where you're going, how you're feeling, your expectations, etc.

While you're there, you can go undercover and try to fit in, or you can tell people why you're there and chat with them about their culture. It's up to you.

When you get home, journal about how it all went.

- How did people react to you?
- How did you feel?
- What did you learn about this culture?
- What did you discover about yourself?

This can be a scary exercise, but with the right attitude, it can be great fun. Be brave. Don't fight the awkward feelings that might come. Let yourself feel them.

And when you're finished, reward yourself for your bravery!

The above exercise gives you a taste of what it's like to travel to a foreign place. Being foreign can ignite a swirl of emotions, both positive and negative – excitement, fascination, awkwardness, fear, the urge to dive in, or the urge to flee.

Writing about these emotions – our reactions to a new place, and our reactions to ourselves in that place – teaches us a lot about our core personalities. We discover who we are beneath the habits, customs, and rules we've learned throughout life. It also adds fun insight to our travel experiences, as we examine the quirks and idiosyncrasies of the places we visit, and contrast them with our own quirks and idiosyncrasies.

You don't have to limit that exercise to your own community. I promised you an excuse for a road trip. That exercise also works great as a day trip out of town. Often the cultural landscape changes quickly once we hit the road. An hour or two from where we live, we often encounter all sorts of people whose ways of thinking and living are different from ours.

Traveling across your own country can also put you in touch with cultures that are foreign to you. When I visited a friend who had moved from Seattle to Tulsa a couple of years ago, she kept apologizing that things weren't like they are in Seattle, but for me it was a cultural adventure. Local dive bars, Wal-Marts, and the campus of Oral Roberts University all showed me worlds I don't normally see.

Hey...I know, let's go to Oklahoma right now. I'll take you shopping for beer....

Dave's Diaries

Tulsa, Oklahoma, U.S.A.

My friend Jeni took me to a liquor store one afternoon in search of beverages of the adult persuasion. As we entered the store, things seemed all wrong. State politics, it turned out, were influencing the store layout. A simple beer run led to this journal entry, which I wrote during my visit, and updated a couple of years later, when Oklahoma changed its liquor laws.

Keeping Cool in Tulsa

I felt perplexed as soon as we walked into the store. The periphery looked just like any other American liquor store, but the middle of the room was cluttered with six-packs and cases – an extensive spectrum of brew – from cans of PBR to bottles of Rochefort and other swanky Belgian ales. The beer was all lined up in neat rows on the floor. None of it was stacked. It was all at ankle level.

"What's with the beer?" I asked Jeni. The on-the-ground display was what one might expect in a poor Third World market, where neither fridges nor shelving were affordable. But even if they didn't have any shelving, why not at least stack the cases on top of each other?

"It's illegal in Oklahoma for liquor stores to refrigerate their beer," Jeni explained. "You can buy cold beer in grocery stores, but it's all 3.2 percent alcohol."

"So? Is it illegal to put the beer on shelves?"

No, Jeni explained. They could do that...but Oklahoma gets hot in the summer. Cement floors stay cool. This one store was making the meager effort they legally could to keep their beer cold.

"They're also not allowed to sell beer on election days," Jeni added as we left, "until after the polls close."

"Huh? They don't want people to vote drunk?"

"I guess not."

Two years later, on the day of the Oklahoma presidential primary, I went to blog about this election day rule. The law seemed so bizarre, I gave Jeni a quick call to be sure I had my facts right.

"I'm not sure if that's still true," she said.

A few minutes later, she e-mailed me, with a link to an article from NewsOK.com, the website for the newspaper *The Oklahoman*. The law, which was enacted in 1959 to stop politicians from bribing voters with booze, had been repealed – just in time for the 2008 presidential primaries.

Postscript

Anecdotes like this one about quirky cultural differences make fun stories for your journal.

- Be careful shopping for toothpaste in Norway. That "toothpaste" tube might actually contain mayonnaise or caviar.
- In Samoa, many local buses have no side windows, offering a wind-in-your-hair ride with "natural air conditioning."
- In Australia, "paper" money is now made of a special paper-like plastic. Why? According to Aussie travelers I've met, it's because they spend so much time at the beach, and ocean water was ruining their old currency.
- In China, it's a bad omen to flip a fish over on your dinner plate. If you do, according to legend, the next fishing boat to pass by will capsize.
- When Danes drink beer, they are especially fond of a little something extra on the side. These little glasses of what they call "snaps" (the Danish word for "schnapps," which we stole from the Germans) come in all sorts of varieties. Traditional examples include akvavit – a potato-based liquor infused with caraway or other herbs, or Gammel Dansk – a Danish bitter

made from a secret recipe. Recently, however, less traditional drams with licorice candy or even Fisherman's Friend cough drops infused into vodka have become trendy.

- People consume more 7-Eleven Slurpees in chilly Winnipeg, Manitoba, Canada, than anywhere else in the world. According to the Canadian Broadcasting Corporation, some residents even go out in their pajamas on Christmas morning for a cup of the fruit-flavored slush. (You'd think they could make their own with a cupful of snow and some juice!)

As you travel, be on the lookout for fun journaling blurbs like these! You can work them into longer entries, or just jot them down quickly as random thoughts.

CHAPTER 7

The Inner Journey

Travel as a Backdrop for Self-Discovery

At the start of this book, I mentioned my crazy, low-budget odyssey through Europe at age 20. I began in Iceland. Then I flew to the northern tip of Norway, where I began winding my way southward on trains, buses, and boats, until three months later I'd made it to southern Turkey. I traveled alone on 26 bucks a day. I had friends in a few places who offered me couches to crash on. Elsewhere, I slept in youth hostels and pensions, on beaches, trains, and train station floors. I journaled fanatically on that trip, stealing moments to write whenever and wherever I could. I returned home with six notebooks full of words.

In the beginning I focused my journaling on the cultures I visited. As I got deeper into my journey, however, I realized my trip wasn't just about exploring Europe. It was also about exploring myself.

Nothing unusual was happening in Europe. The year was 1989, and Europe was doing what it had been doing for years. Iceland's volcanoes were steaming. Berlin's Wall was dividing.

In Paris, that Mona Lisa chick was smiling.* In Greece, friends gathered each night in the tavernas to eat souvlaki and drink retsina like they always did. And in Norway, the fjords were doing...well, whatever it is that fjords do – being "beautiful," I suppose. Even though much of what I saw was new to my own personal experience, these were everyday occurrences in the places where they were happening. I was experiencing normal, everyday life. It just wasn't *my* normal, everyday life. The differences I thought were around me were really within me.

*Or grimacing. She's never looked too happy to me, and hey, I'd be cranky too if I had to spend every day on display in the Louvre with a horde of tourists gawking at me.

In high school, I'd been an insecure kid. I had grown up in a community that reeked of cliquishness. When I went away to college, I lugged my insecurities with me. My childhood self-doubt still loomed over me like a cranky monster, big and growling. On my trip through Europe, everything changed. Finally, at age 20, I began feeling comfortable with who I was. After several weeks away from my familiar world, my uptight personality started to relax. Just as I was free to wander wherever I wanted in Europe, I began feeling free to wander where I wanted within my own mind. I stopped worrying so much about pleasing other people or making a good impression. Ironically, once I did this, I think people started to like me better. More importantly, I started to like myself better.

It took a radical change in my surroundings – an exhausting, three-month, solo journey – to jolt me out of my childhood insecurities. I returned from Europe with newfound confidence.

The trip changed my life, but it wasn't just the journey. It was the fact that I wrote it down. I am 100 percent convinced if I hadn't journaled during this trip, much of my new understanding about who I was, how I thought, and the new ways I wanted to begin thinking would have been lost. Back in familiar surroundings, it would have been easy to default back to my old self.

Travel changes us – not always as profoundly as this particular journey did for me, but whenever we venture into new territory, we expose ourselves to new ideas, and we evolve based on those ideas. When we return home, though, it's easy and natural to revert to our previous selves. Short moments of self-discovery in faraway places get covered up by the static of everyday life as we fall back into old routines.

Journaling about these self-discoveries puts us better in touch with them. Why? When we write – even when we write fast, as we do if we speed journal – we slow down our thinking. It's like walking through a park versus driving past a park. Which way will you get a closer look at the park? In this sense, even if you never even read your journals after a trip is over, you will still benefit from writing about your inner journey.

Looking Inside

The physical newness of an unfamiliar place can distract us to the point that we either forget or don't bother to write about our emotions. Besides, let's be realistic: The outer journey is what motivates us to travel. We go to China to see the Great Wall, gobble dim sum, or meet the people – not because we're searching for earth-shattering discoveries about our personalities. We travel to get away from our everyday stresses and concerns, so delving into our thoughts might seem like it could drag a trip down. But if you do it right, it won't.

Journaling about your emotions – positive and negative – can add profound insight to your journeys. It can diminish the negative energy and stress you might otherwise carry on a vacation. Write down your more prickly thoughts with the right approach, and you might find yourself laughing about incidents that would otherwise annoy you.

Flight Simulator

An Emotional Inventory

Think for a moment about your past travels – or about upcoming travels or trips you hope to one day take. Then, list as many emotions as you can think of that might be stirred up because you're away from home. When you think you're done, sit with your list for a few more minutes. See if anything else is slow to emerge.

After you make your list, sort your emotions into two groups – positive and negative – and jot down which emotions fall into which category. Some emotions might fall into both categories. Others might seem neutral – neither positive nor negative. If an emotion falls into both categories, or if one is difficult to categorize either way, make a note of that.

Travel amplifies certain emotions. It sparks others that might lie dormant at home. These amped-up emotions are all part of culture shock. That term, "culture shock," often has negative connotations, but many emotions we experience as a part of culture shock are positive.

Curiosity or excitement about our new surroundings, pride that we've accomplished a task or taken on new challenges, peace or relaxation away from our everyday stresses, a sense of wonder – that "pinch me, I must be snoring and drooling all over my pillow" feeling – as we revel in the newness of a location; these are all endorphin-tickling emotions that get stirred up in unfamiliar places.

Then there are the not-so-pleasant emotions. Confusion, frustration, embarrassment, prejudice, and anger can rear their ugly heads when we're out of our element. Sometimes we don't like the thoughts that flow through our minds. Away from our everyday environments, things don't always work as we expect them to. People behave differently. Technology operates differently. Sometimes when we travel, we feel like we don't know what we're doing, and this can make us cranky.

Emotions that feel good are easier to journal about than emotions that don't. If you ignore your not-so-pleasant emotions, however, you short-change yourself. For one thing, when writers hold back and omit details, their words sound vacant. There's a hole in their stories. On a more personal level, if you ignore your not-so-nice emotions when you write, you miss opportunities to diffuse or reverse them.

We're now going to look at ways to write about all of your emotions – even the ones that make you want to scream and throw stuff. In a little while, we'll look at those trickier feelings, but I'm going to ease you into things first with the fun parts of the inner journey.

The Showing Must Go On!

Just as you scan all of your senses before writing about your outer journey, take a quick emotional inventory before you write about your inner journey. List in your mind all of the different emotions you felt during the scene you're about to cover. Picture yourself back there, and take a moment to search for the quieter emotions you felt. Just as one particular sense might be dominant in the outer journey, the same can happen with your inner journey. Other, subtler emotions may be lurking beneath the surface.

Stick with the "Show, don't tell" rule. Just as writing, "The fjords are beautiful," doesn't paint a picture of what the fjords really look like, neither does writing, "I'm so excited."

Why are you excited? Are you feeling a sense of accomplishment at finding your way around a new place? Thrilled about finally arriving at a destination you've dreamed about for years?

Are you proud you've just eaten a local specialty you didn't think you'd be able to choke down?* Or maybe you're just excited because your crotchety boss is far, far away. Whatever reasons lie behind your feelings, write them down.

*I was once tricked into eating spicy lamb intestines. Not knowing what they were, I went back for seconds.

Elaborate. If you've written, "I can't believe I'm finally here," ask yourself why. What did you go through to get to this place? What does being there mean to you? Stretch your emotional descriptions and weave them together with things you've done. Have you accomplished a physical challenge? Climbed a mountain, or conquered the local transportation system? Maybe you got lost looking for a hotel, and had an adventure along the way. Have you done something that your friends back home would think was rock-star-esque? How does it feel to have this accomplishment, far from the people who know you, where none of them can see what you're doing?

Go beyond the "big picture" of what you're experiencing too. Write down your little victories. Seeing the sights, finding the ideal beach, or discovering your new favorite restaurant on the planet are all journal-worthy, but sometimes, smaller, momentary events deserve written celebrations.

Working as a tour guide in France, I had a man on my tour run up to me one afternoon with a gaping grin on his face. "Dave!" he said, "I went into a shop and said '*bonjour*' to the shopkeeper and he said '*bonjour*' back to me!"

I stood there, waiting for the rest of the story. Then it dawned on me; there was no rest of the story. That was it. I was used to dealing with language barriers, so having a Frenchman utter, "*bonjour,*" hardly seemed earth-shattering – but then I realized: this man had never uttered a non-English word in his life. For him, to make a connection with a Parisian in the local language was one of the coolest things he had ever done. He had snuck one little toe across the language barrier for the first time in his life...and it worked! For the rest of the day, he wallowed in his victory.

If you do something you think is cool, gloat. Yes, people get annoyed with gloaters, which is why your private journal is the perfect place for such behavior. Your notebook pages won't roll their eyes at you. Years later, when you read about these moments, you'll be reminded how ultra-cool you were while traveling. And that ultra-coolness just might spill over into life at home.

Really? Why?

Travel makes us cranky sometimes too. Travel is meant to be fun – and most of it is – but think of all the things we have to contend with: fatigue and jet lag, aching feet, confusion about the local way of doing things, language barriers, forgotten toothbrushes, currency conversions, and the ubiquitous International Toilet of Mystery, which we can't figure out how to flush. When we wander into unfamiliar turf, all sorts of things can throw our moods into grump-mode. Journaling about these things helps tame your inner travel grump.

Now, I know writing down negative travel attitudes might not sound productive. A handful of travelers experience a megadose of perceived "problems," and their journeys become traveling whinefests. Most of us don't want to be like that. But this isn't about looking for reasons to gripe. It's about getting to the root of what's bugging you, and sorting it out on paper so you can get on with your trip without dwelling. The trick is doing it in a constructive way.

If you're feeling cranky, the two questions, "Really?" and "Why?" can work wonders in de-crankifying you. How? I'll start out with a goofy example. For the sake of metaphor, let's take a closer look at the aforementioned International Toilet of Mystery. It's a common frustration among international travelers: You've just used a toilet in a faraway land. Now you find yourself staring at the toilet, baffled by how to flush. Is there a handle to jiggle? A button to push? A cord to pull? A foot pedal? You can't find any of those. Maybe you're just supposed to kick the toilet and shout, "Toilet, I command you to flush!"* You want to flush this mystery toilet, but you can't. It is unlike any toilet you have ever encountered, and no matter what you do, the toilet won't flush. You get annoyed.

*For the record, I have never found this method to be successful.

Stupid toilet!

So what's up? How are you feeling?

"I'm annoyed."

Why?

"I'm annoyed because this stupid toilet won't flush!"

Oh really? The toilet is stupid?

"Okay, fine. I'm annoyed because the stupid people in this stupid country don't know how to make a toilet that flushes properly."

Really? Millions of people in this country probably use toilets like this one every day. And they probably manage to flush them just fine.

"All right. I'm annoyed because I don't know how to flush this toilet."

And why does that annoy you?

"Because, dude, I've known how to flush a toilet since I was, like, two or three years old!"

Now we're getting somewhere.

Our annoyance is a secondary emotion. What we're really feeling, over something as trivial as flushing a toilet, is helplessness. Yeah, I know "helpless" is a strong word to attach to a little bathroom stress, but it's what our mind is perceiving. When we travel, we often encounter situations where we don't know how to do something we've taken for granted for years, such as flush a toilet, read a menu, count our change, or decipher a bus schedule. This sudden loss of a normally mundane skill can make us a little crazed. And it's natural to blame our new surroundings. The helplessness we feel is usually a *sense* of helplessness, however – not real helplessness. We find solutions – even if it means walking away from that unflushed toilet. But in the moment, not understanding the local way things are done can leave us feeling rattled. Journaling about these things helps us realize they're not that big a deal. And, irritating as they can be while they are happening, they can end up being some of our favorite travel stories later.

I've had a rule about travel for many years. "When you travel, things go wrong." Outside our usual environments, it's inevitable things will get wonky at times. What we often don't realize in the moment is these frustrating incidents can make for hilarious memories. When we get home, distant from the events, we giggle as we reread our descriptions. Write your frustrations into your journals, but challenge yourself as you do. You can turn your more challenging travel moments into laughter-inducing tales.

I'm not suggesting you journal about every toilet experience you have while traveling (though it can be a fun theme journaling topic). The unflushable toilet is my extremely mature metaphor for all the things that bug us when we travel. Start journaling about these things, asking yourself "Why?" and "Really?" as you go, and you just might write your way into a calmer state of mind. You don't need to actually write the back-and-forth dialogue we had in the previous example, but go through it in your mind as you journal.

All right...enough ranting about stupid toilets. I've got one more example I'd like to share with you – a serious story about a mean person who threatened to kill me, and how journaling helped me laugh at the guy later.

Lessons from a Bad Guy

In my mid 20s, on my first trip to Portugal, I was robbed less than two hours after my plane landed. It happened in Lisbon on a crowded street in broad daylight. A man came up to me and demanded money. I refused to give him any.

He became aggressive. He got in my face. He told me his friend had just been released from prison and was watching us from somewhere in the crowd. If I didn't give him 5,000 escudos (this was before the Euro currency existed), if I tried to run or yell for help, he said he and his friend would follow me to my hotel and kill me.

It was a sunny day on a pedestrian street packed with people. Two blocks earlier, I had seen a couple of policemen. I tried to turn around and walk in their direction, but the man blocked my path. In the end, I decided getting myself killed would not be a fun cultural experience. I emptied my wallet of the 9,000 escudos I had in cash. Nine thousand escudos, I calculated, were worth about five dollars and 60 cents. My life was worth at least that much.

After the robber disappeared into the crowd, I revisited my exchange rate calculations. I had been thinking in Italian lira, not Portuguese escudos. Nine thousand escudos were worth 56 dollars, not $5.60.

Intimidated and shaken, I slithered back to my hotel. I felt vulnerable, paranoid, and angry – angry at the guy who robbed me, even more angry at myself. I'd just been ripped off on a crowded street in broad daylight. Was I that much of a pushover to believe this man was really going to kill me? Surely it was just a scare tactic. I should have run, or made a scene, rather than sheepishly handing over my cash.

I beat myself up about this for days. I even had nightmares – until I started asking myself those two questions: "Really?" and "Why?"

Why was I angry at the man? Because he robbed me. Why was I angry that he robbed me? Because robbing people is wrong and he shouldn't have done that. Really? Maybe he had a family to feed. Maybe he couldn't find work and his children were starving. And yeah, he'd threatened me, but he hadn't hurt me. How many parents would rob somebody in order to save their own child's life? Most.

Oh, but come on! Was he *really* robbing me to save his child's life? Probably not. Nevertheless, my anger at him wasn't doing the world any good. All it was doing was making my own vacation miserable.

Why was I angry at myself? I should have defended myself better. Really? Maybe he really *would* have hurt me. Why else was I angry at myself? I was too submissive. I acted like a coward. Really? Would a coward board an airplane by himself and fly across eight time zones to a country where he didn't speak the language, didn't know anyone, didn't know his way around? Would a coward start out his explorations of a new city in the part of town his guidebook warned was the rough part of town, simply because he thought that part of town sounded culturally fascinating?*

*Ironically, I was robbed right after I left the so-called "rough" neighborhood.

Oh yeah...then, there were a couple of other little details in reality that I had conveniently omitted from the self-effacing story I was trapped in. Minutes before I was robbed, I had just gone into a bank to change money. I had 9,000 escudos in my wallet, but I had another 40,000 escudos – 250 dollars – stashed beneath my clothing in my moneybelt. And that wasn't all. In 10 days, I was scheduled to meet up with another tour guide in Paris. I had been asked to carry a large sum of tour funds over to him – 7,000 dollars in unsigned travelers checks. Seven thousand dollars! Unsigned travelers checks were as good as cash.

The robber had put me on the spot, forced me to make a split-second decision. *Of course,* while he was demanding to see how much cash was in my wallet, I was screamingly aware of the huge wad of money stashed under my clothing. I had made a quick mathematical miscalculation – a mistake anyone could make in a moment like this – and opted to surrender what I thought was $5.60 in order to avert the possibility of losing (1) 7,000 dollars, and (2) my life.

Had I *really* been a coward? No way, man! I'd been a freaking genius! If only this loser knew what he missed out on! After journaling about the incident, guided by the questions, "Really?" and "Why?" I found myself cackling with laughter. *Bwahahahahaaaa!*

What did I learn from this confrontation? Well, for starters, I learned to never carry that much cash again.*

*The company I was guiding for no longer allows its employees to transport money for other guides, so if you see me on the streets of some foreign city and are thinking of whacking me, don't waste your energy, okay?

But I learned something bigger than that too: My negative emotions were based on my surface version of the truth. Once I started dissecting those emotions with my two questions, I realized that under the circumstances, the way I dealt with the robber had been just fine.

I journaled my way out of the recording in my head that kept telling me to be angry and sulky. I had a much better trip after that.

So to recap:

- Journal about your thoughts and feelings because they will make your travel diaries more interesting.
- Journal about your thoughts and feelings because they will make your travels happier.
- Do not try to rob me. I am a struggling

freelance writer, and I will poke you in
the eye with my pencil.*

*It's an automatic, bolt-action pencil with aerodynamic lines and a clip for easy concealment. James Bond asked to borrow it.

Body Language

One last thing worth looking at when writing about your inner journey is how your body feels in the moment. Emotions evoke physical responses. Your muscles tense or relax. Your heart beats faster or slower. Your skin tingles. Your hands shiver. You let out a sigh, or a shriek. You give a hug or a high five to your travel partner. These things too show how you are feeling.

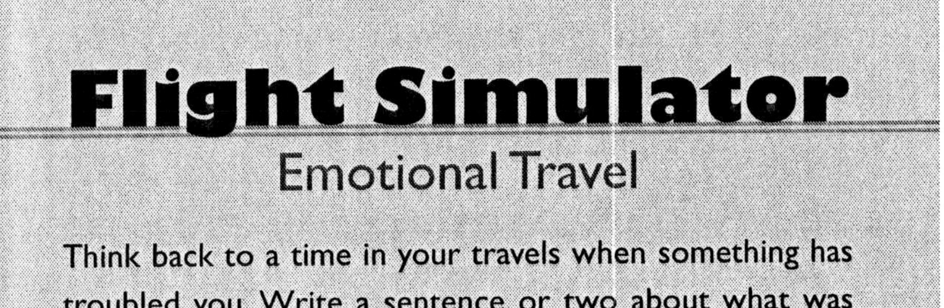

Flight Simulator

Emotional Travel

Think back to a time in your travels when something has troubled you. Write a sentence or two about what was bothering you during this experience. Then – using the questions, "Really?" and "Why?" – speed journal for 10 minutes about the event and how you felt. Ask yourself those questions every couple of sentences. When you're finished, keep reading.

Uncovering the Truth

Did you discover anything about your thoughts in the previous exercise? Did anything you wrote surprise you? When we write fast and fearlessly enough that we don't censor our thoughts, big revelations sometimes bubble to the surface.

The first time you do this exercise, it might or might not lead you to such revelations. Sometimes, other forces at play in our minds hinder us from getting at the real truth right away.

This sort of journaling is a time when our Inner Censors tend to go on rampages. If you're getting mental postcards, text messages, collect calls, or smoke signals from your Inner Censor, remember you have sent him or her far away, and you don't have to listen.

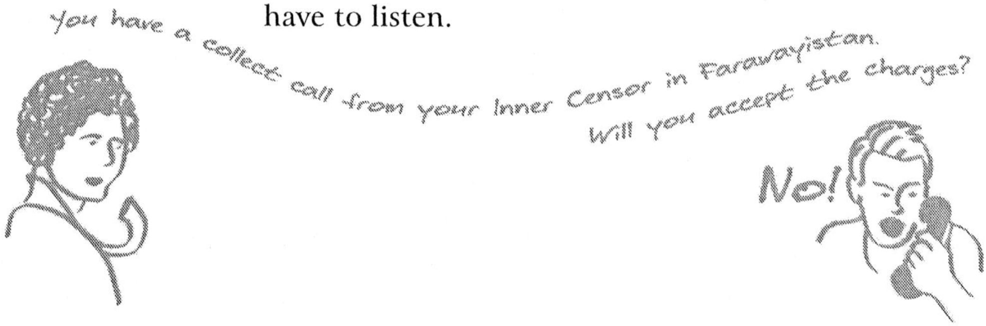

Coming Up for Air

There's one final thing I want to mention about writing down your inner journey. I don't want you to have a nervous breakdown on your vacation. Vacations are supposed to help us avoid such incidents.

Some people carry around big personal issues – traumatic events or experiences they haven't fully processed. Journaling about these things can be an effective way to confront them, but you might not want to get into intense, long-term personal issues when you're far from people who care about you. As you journal and explore your deeper emotions, you might stumble upon things in your brain that are better set aside until you get home. If this happens, make a note of them. You could even send yourself a postcard to be sure they don't sink back down into your mental muck and stay there. But it's okay to leave these issues alone while traveling. If you're in an exciting foreign place, let yourself have fun.

Dave's Diaries

Ankara, Turkey
(written in Madison, Wisconsin)

My most frightening travel experience ever happened on my second visit to Turkey. On my first trip, I fell in love with the country. Four years later, when I moved to Ankara to teach English, things didn't go so well.

A few weeks into my stay, I was hospitalized with a nasty intestinal parasite. Excellent health care was available in Ankara, but unbeknownst to me at the time, I was taken to a hospital with a horrible reputation.

I arrived at the hospital too weak to walk, barely able to speak, shivering uncontrollably from severe dehydration. The emergency room was ghastly, crammed with beds, each of which contained the victim of either a similar stomach ailment or a car crash. When doctors led me to my own bed, the first thing I noticed was a large blood stain on the sheets. Too weak to protest, I lay down and closed my eyes.

A few weeks later, suffering from a variety of secondary infections and severe weight loss, I came whimpering home to Wisconsin. I felt depressed and demoralized. Most of all, I felt ashamed. I'd lived in Turkey less than two months when my goal had been to stay two years. Among my friends, I had always been the intrepid traveler. That had been my identity, and temporarily, I had met my downfall.

Depression from the experience echoed for months afterward. Then one day – safe and healthy again, but still reeling emotionally – I did some speed journaling. As I wrote, I questioned the story I'd been telling myself about what had happened. Ten minutes of writing brought a truer story to light, and helped me make peace with everything that happened on that trip.

Now, with apologies to my mother and anyone else who might be shocked by a few choice words in the following paragraphs (hey, like I said, we should never censor ourselves when speed journaling), here is the unedited, uncensored, original version of what I wrote 15 years ago, in a 10-minute journaling blast, along with an epilogue of what happened after I wrote:

My Most Traumatic Travel Experience Ever ...And How Journaling Helped Me Travel Again

Blood stains on my sheets. That's what I remember most – that's what I tell people about now – because perhaps I can fool them into thinking my life really WAS in danger. Blood-stained sheets in a Turkish hospital bed, but it's not my own blood. And lying in a bloody hospital bed and it's someone else's blood makes other people – who listen to me recount this story – think of AIDS. And AIDS makes them think of death.

But I wasn't dying. And the blood was dry. It couldn't hurt me. Could it? The IV in my arm was clean. I knew it was clean because I made Phillip [my roommate] watch them put it in – after they unwrapped its sealed package.

I was scared. Shit, was I scared! I don't know if I'd ever been more scared. When I caught the word, "cholera," in amongst the doctor's Turkish babble, I was really fucking scared. But I was never anywhere close to death. Why do I look back now and think I was being a wimp through the whole thing?

It's incredible – I was only half conscious. They had to carry me down the stairs to the taxi. I was too weak to yell for help, even. So how the hell can it be so vivid in my mind now? How can so many details be there? Like the damn cigarette smoke Phil kept spewing in my face as the taxi driver – on a macho medical emergency fantasy – sped through Ankara flashing his lights, honking his horn, blasting that damn music. What was going on with me that night?

I had always talked tough. If I traveled long enough, I'd get sick. It was all part of the game. But when it really finally happened to me, it wasn't a game anymore. It wasn't an adventure. And I felt defeated.

Postscript

In the 10 minutes I spent on this exercise, I didn't have time to reach the full conclusion I was headed toward, but my writing pointed me in the right direction. In the days that followed, as I processed what I had written, I came to understand what had really happened in Turkey. I had been through a traumatic travel experience. I had been sufficiently ill that for the first time in my life, rational or not, I had feared I might die. I'd been taken to a hospital that was not up to good sanitary standards, where not a single doctor spoke any language I could speak. And yeah, the blood-stained sheets were one of several things that had spooked me, but once I speed journaled about the experience, I came to a new understanding of the realities of that night.

My sheets were clean. They had been sterilized. Blood stains are hard to wash out, and an American hospital would have disposed of them. But really, lying down in that bed hadn't put my health in further jeopardy. "My sheets were bloodstained" elicited more shock and sympathy from friends, however, than "I had diarrhea." So I was running around telling everybody about the blood stains – and beating myself up at the same time for overdramatizing the situation.

Journaling about the experience, with a focus on my emotions, I began to understand the fear I had felt. I began to give myself a break. I had gone through a frightening experience and encountered some mysterious medical problems. In addition to my sad state of physical health, I had become emotionally exhausted. I had done what I needed to do, and come home.

I had encountered a rare moment in travel when the best thing to do was bail, regroup, and start again when I was healthy. That was reality. No embellishments were necessary.

Journaling about this experience helped me arrive at a deeper truth. The blood-stained sheets had been my melodramatic metaphor for the struggle I had been through. I had exaggerated the situation in my mind to cover up my sense of failure. But I hadn't "failed." I had been very unlucky. It was time to stop overdramatizing. It was time to start traveling again.

And I did.

Obviously, I wasn't laughing at the time; however, years after the experience, having made peace with the ordeal, I would write about it again from a humorous perspective. To write my way out of depression, and then turn the story into something funny, was one of my biggest journaling triumphs.

[You'll find the lighter version of this story, "When Salads Attack," in my book of travel humor essays – *Getting Lost: Mishaps of an Accidental Nomad.*]

CHAPTER 8

Travel Journaling When You're Not Traveling

Pre-Journaling, Post-Journaling, and Re-Journaling

Traveling can be a frustrating hobby. Most hobbies are things you can do spontaneously on random Saturdays or Tuesday nights – things that don't require a lot of advance planning, like playing an instrument or sport, knitting, collecting bottle caps, or toilet papering your neighbors' trees. Travel doesn't generally allow such spontaneity. But with all due respect to the bottle cap collectors of the world, I'd rather devote my free time to chasing down foreign cultures, even if I can only do it sporadically.*

*And my neighbors get cranky when I toilet paper their trees.

We've all got things in life that slow down our travel goals. Jobs or school, family commitments, and money issues make it hard to just hop a flight to Burkina Faso for the weekend. But with journaling methods I'll teach you now, you can quench your traveler's thirst and take mini-vacations with the Ghost of Travels Past and the Ghost of Travels Yet-to-Come. Through techniques I call Pre-Journaling, Post-Journaling, and Re-Journaling, you can write some of your most thought-provoking journal entries from the mundane safety of your kitchen table.

Sure, journaling from home isn't the same as being there, but it provides an outlet for all that stray energy you might have kicking around – that "I need to go somewhere *now!*" feeling we get when we've been home too long. Writing about your travels before and after they happen also adds broader perspective to your journals, offering a deeper understanding of how your travels transform you.

Pre-Journaling

Pre-journaling is writing about a trip before you ever leave home. What's the point to that? Big trips change us. By the time we embark on an adventure, we've spent weeks, months, even years, dreaming and planning. We've fantasized about the scenery, the food, the people we'll meet. We've read about the sights we want to see, plotted how to get around, pictured our accommodations. We've bought guidebooks, scoured maps, and made reservations. Write about those preparations. They're a big part of your journey.

As we prepare to go into unknown territory, we experience all sorts of emotions too, from giddy anticipation to nervous uncertainty. What are you looking forward to? What are you anxious about? These sorts of things are the inner-journey part of pre-journaling. And what about your expectations of what a place will be like? Our expectations ahead of time color the ways we react to places once we're there. So journal too about any preconceptions you might have.

When I suggest this in my classes, someone invariably raises their hand and says, "But Dave, I travel without expectations! It's wrong to travel with expectations! You shouldn't judge places you've never been to!"

Oh, come on! Being non-judgmental is super. You're pro-world-peace? Most excellent! Here, have a gold star. But you travel to places with *no clue whatsoever* of what they're like?! If you didn't have *some* picture in your mind of what a place was like, why would you go there in the first place? You wouldn't even know what to pack.

We all travel with preconceptions. We need preconceptions. These vague ideas of what life is like in any particular part of the world are what nudge us to go. They help us pick our destinations. But when we arrive, we often discover the vague ideas we had don't jibe with reality. Things look different, sound different, smell different, even feel different from what we anticipated. Journaling ahead of time about your trip helps contrast your pre-journey expectations with the realities you encounter once you're there. It helps you process any culture shock you might experience, and it adds focus to your trip planning.

Flight Simulator

A Journey Is Born

Journeys don't begin at the point of departure. They start much more subtly, long before we begin traveling. Sometimes, we're not even aware at first that a new travel dream is gurgling within us. But the dream slowly grows, kicking and burping until we can't ignore it. You've probably got several journeys under way in your mind right now.

Sit for a couple of minutes and make a list of all the places in the world you'd like to visit. Don't worry about whether or not you can go there anytime soon. Fantasize. Let your brain take a quick lap around the globe, and jot down some dream destinations.

Once you've listed at least seven or eight places (or if you are like me, 2,758 destinations), pick one, and picture yourself there. Imagine your arrival. Imagine yourself walking through this place. In your mind, really try to be there.

Now, write for 10 to 20 minutes about the place you've chosen. As you write, answer the following questions:

- Why do you want to go there? What interests you about this place?
- How easy or difficult would it be to actually go? Is there anything that hinders you from going?
- What can you do to make this trip happen, in spite of any perceived hindrances – if not right away, then maybe in the future?
- What do you expect your outer journey will be like when you get there? What will things look like? What will you do? What will the people be like?
- What about your inner journey? How do you think you will react to this place? What emotions might you experience?

Whenever I think about an upcoming adventure in a new place, I get a floaty sensation. My adrenaline kicks in. Sometimes I even get a mild head rush. If you notice similar sensations within yourself, an adventure is already alive inside of you.

Even if you don't have this sort of reaction, dreaming about your next trip, the preceding exercise serves a couple of purposes. Once you arrive in a new place, having pre-journaled about it, you'll have a richer perspective on why you're there. More importantly, journaling about a fantasy trip – *especially* a trip you don't think you'd ever be able to take – can be a step toward making that journey happen.

All sorts of situations in life hinder us from traveling – lack of money, lack of time, physical challenges, and sometimes, plain and simple fear. Dreams that go unfulfilled, however, tend to gnaw at us. Writing about a journey you've fantasized about just might be the first step in making the trip happen.

Post-Journaling

So if pre-journaling is writing about a trip before it happens, then post-journaling must be…anybody? Yes, I see a hand. You, over there…yes, you, reading the book. Thank you for volunteering. What do you suppose post-journaling is?

(Please insert answer here.)

Exactly! Post-journaling is writing about a journey after it's finished! My, aren't you intelligent!*

*Oh, and by the way, that book you're reading looks fascinating!

If you've been doing all the exercises as you make your way through this book, you've already done some post-journaling. Post-journaling satisfies travel cravings in a different way from pre-journaling. It carries us back to places we've been. If you find yourself itching to relive a travel experience, unable to go there at the immediate moment, post-journaling will help quell those twitchy sensations we get when we're stuck at home too long.

That's not all. You know all those trips you've taken in the past where you wish you had kept a better journal? Well, it's not too late. People assume if they don't write their journals while they're traveling, they can't do it later. But journaling has no deadlines. There are no late fees, no penalties if you forget to file for an extension. You can write about a trip years after it's finished.

One nice thing about travel journaling at home is we don't have the same time pressure we encounter on the road. You can slow things down now, ponder your words at a leisurely pace before setting them on paper. If you like speed journaling, that works at home too, but if you want to slow down, now is the time.

With one exception….

What's the biggest challenge in journaling about a trip that happened long ago? Remembering. Many people think post-journaling about a long-ago journey is impossible because so many details have left them. Speed journaling can bring those details back. Often there's a snowball effect. One tiny memory triggers a bigger memory, and so on, until suddenly, your mind is fully immersed in your long-ago-and-far-away journey.*

I will remember

*If you need to bring your mind back home, just click your heels together and...yeah, you know the drill.

If you're wanting to journal about a trip that's far in the past, and the memories don't seem to be coming, begin with 10 minutes of speed journaling. Start with the words, "I remember," and let things flow from there. See what tumbles onto your pages. Then, if you like, slow down and shape your words into something more literary.

What fascinates me when I post-journal is how much my perspective changes once I've returned home. Take my earlier Turkish hospital story, for example. I was too sickly and depressed to journal much about the experience while it was happening, but I remember clearly what I was thinking and how I felt. Had I written more while I was there, I would have written with complete sincerity that I feared my life was in danger, that my dream of traveling the world was crumbling into an utter failure, and that I was about to go whimpering back home where my friends would be dreadfully disappointed in me. Speed journaling about the experience several months after the fact, I had a fresh perspective. I was home – healthy, safe, over the worst of my depression, and able to take a gigantic, trans-Atlantic step back from the experience – to write with a different, more realistic perspective.

Flight Simulator

Going Back

You probably have at least one trip in your past where you either didn't journal at all, or you did journal, but not in the ways you wish you would have. Let's do something about that.

Choose a place you've already visited. It can be a far-away place you've only been once, or someplace closer to home where you've been many times. Once you've chosen your place, try to identify a specific moment, day, or event in that place. Speed journal about that moment for 10 minutes or more, and watch how many memories come back. As a launching pad, use the words, "I remember...."

Once you recall a couple of details, other memories that you've squished deeper in your subconscious mind will likely reveal themselves. Run with them in whatever direction they take you.

After you've gotten the basics down in a 10-minute writing spree, you can hit the brakes and rewrite at a more leisurely pace, filling in details and polishing your words into a well-written essay.

Return to Hammamet

I had one of my most powerful journaling experiences on a trip to northern Africa a few years ago. Writing at home before my trip, I was both pre-journaling and post-journaling at the same time.

In 1976, when my family was living in England, we spent Christmas in Tunisia. I was eight years old. My brother, Steve, was four. We took off from Heathrow Airport on a chilly London night. Four hours later, as we touched down in Tunis, I was plunged into the most amazing culture shock my young mind had ever experienced.

We spent a week in Hammamet, a coastal village of dirt roads and palm trees. We made day trips to Muslim holy cities, rode camels on the beach, and drank tea in the spartan home of an orange farmer.

After we moved back to America, Hammamet swirled in my mind like a surreal dream. My memories faded with age, but they never vanished. My entire childhood year living in England was memorable, but our week in Tunisia stood out. Everything had been so radically different that week from any other week I had ever lived. I longed to return and experience it again.

By my mid-20s, Tunisia had become a strange part of me I needed to reconnect with. It was so far in the past, I began at times to question whether I had even been there. I had the passport stamp to prove it, but the memory was hard to believe. I needed to go back and prove to myself I hadn't made the whole thing up.

Before leaving America, I sat down to pre-journal about my upcoming trip. As I began writing about my expectations, I realized they were all based on memories. The tricky thing was I wasn't sure how many of my memories were accurate, and how many were images I had concocted in my mind.

I remembered towns we had visited on day trips – little bits and pieces at least – but the details had blurred together into one coagulated glob. So I stopped trying to recapture the journey in any sort of chronological order. I just began spilling random thoughts onto the page.

My journal entry became a scrawled list of memories: riding camels on the beach, women in veils, stray cats at our hotel, an excruciating leg cramp on Christmas Eve, bottled water – a brand called Safia, pink Safia bottle caps with a red logo in Roman and Arabic script,* a three-foot-tall man in a fez who

*I really did collect bottle caps then

made change for the hotel's pinball machines, palm trees, pungent food in olive oil that my eight-year-old taste buds hated, the Muslim call to prayer billowing from minarets, walking along the beach with my mom on the day my dad was sick with food poisoning, the walled city nearby, a beggar with deformed feet who passed his time at the city gates.

That last memory, of the beggar, popped into my mind suddenly. I hadn't thought about him in years, but I could picture him now, gesturing down at his deformed feet, which pointed inward toward each other instead of forward.

My list went on and on. I wrote myself into a frenzy, losing track of time. One detail triggered another. Two hours later, my trip from 20 years earlier was down on paper. Finally it felt real again.

I remembered the hotel we stayed in. It had been our home for a week. I remembered the courtyard, and my brother's obsession with the stray cats that hung out there. I remembered a friendly waiter in the hotel restaurant who winced when I refused to eat the food. Now I wanted not just to go back to Hammamet, but to stay in the same hotel. Could I find it?

Here kitty, kitty...

I phoned my mom to ask if perhaps she had written the name down somewhere. "Oh," she remembered nonchalantly, as if our trip had been a week ago, "it's called the Fourati."

I wrote to the Tunisian embassy in Washington, DC, and asked if they had heard of the hotel, if it even still existed. Two weeks later, I received a response:

"The Hotel Fourati is now the biggest hotel in Hammamet. You will find that Hammamet has changed considerably since your visit in 1977. Tunisia's tourism industry has made great strides, and Hammamet is now a popular resort town."

A resort town? I recalled dirt roads and only a couple of hotels. I didn't want to go to Tunisia to hang out in a resort. But I had to stay at the Fourati. It was beckoning.

On a break between guiding tours in Europe, I hopped an 80-dollar flight from Rome to Tunis and caught a ride down to Hammamet. Walking back into the hotel was like stepping into my own past. Tunisia had come to seem fictitious, but I was there again now, surrounded by it. I was overwhelmed with culture shock, even more so than I had been when visiting with my parents at age eight. But more than culture shock, I was flooded with memories.

The hotel had expanded, but the original buildings were the same. The food had improved slightly, but the desserts still had their familiar, oily flavor. I struck up a conversation with a waiter one evening. He had worked at the hotel when I was there in 1976. Was he the same, friendly man who had hovered over our table two decades before, concerned that I wasn't eating enough? I'll never know for sure, but I believe he was. My most mind-blowing experience, however, came the following day.

I hiked along the beach, just as I had done with my mother 20 years earlier, a couple of kilometers to the medina, the original walled city. Outside the city walls, Hammamet was modern now with paved roads and high-rise hotels. Within the medina, the same shops bustled as they had for centuries.

I approached the city walls and remembered their brown, blocky shape. I recalled teenagers who, 20 years earlier, had tried to sell toy camels to my mother and me for a coin or two. I wondered if the same guys were working in the medina now. As I came to the gate, I saw the beggar.

It was him! The same man I had remembered from 20 years earlier. It had to be him. He was in the same spot as he had sat in 1976, with the same pointed-in feet. I was stunned. I was sure by now he would have been elsewhere, if alive at all. But nearly every day of the last 20 years, he must have sat there, one hand cupped and outstretched, the other hand pointing down at his feet as people walked by.

I wanted to tell him my story, but I was too shy, too afraid it might hurt his feelings that I remembered his feet from 20 years earlier. So I gave him a couple of coins and continued into the bazaar. He nodded and thanked me. He had no idea how he had helped me connect with a small but resilient childhood memory.

Had I not pre-journaled before my trip, I never would have believed this was real. I would have convinced myself it was a weird *déjà vu* experience – that my mind was playing tricks on me, that actually, I was seeing him for the first time and imagining I had seen him on my previous trip. But back in America, in my bedroom in Seattle, were the couple of lines I had scrawled about him. When I returned to my American bedroom several weeks later, the first thing I did was check to be sure I really had journaled about the beggar.

Sometimes, in the moments when we journal, we don't realize the power of what we're writing. Sometimes, we're sending important messages to ourselves, messages whose true value we will discover sometime in the future.

Re-Journaling

Re-journaling is a special kind of post-journaling. It's taking a journal entry we've written while traveling, and rewriting it. But there's more to re-journaling than just revising. Maybe you've been diligently speed journaling throughout your trip. You've come home with reams of beautiful scrawl, hasty handwriting only you can decipher. Now it's time to settle into second drafts, third drafts, eighteenth drafts, and turn those speed journals into the literary masterpieces you wished you had time to write while traveling.

If you feel like doing that, I am proud of you. Seriously, you're making me all misty-eyed here. Re-journaling is something different, however. It's more than just spiffing up and spell-checking your on-the-road rough drafts.

When you re-journal, you take a journal entry you've

already written, and you write about that journal entry. You don't just make it sound prettier. You delve into what you were thinking when you wrote it, and contrast that with the way you feel now.

Here's an example of how re-journaling works: After spending third grade in England, my next trip out of the United States happened just before I was 16. My friend, Anthony, who lived around the corner, was Greek. Every summer, his family went back to Greece. Every year, they invited me to go with them. Finally, after several years of telling me, "Maybe next year," my father sacrificed some hard-earned frequent flier miles, and I was off.

I was going to Greece for culture and sunshine. Something unexpected happened when I arrived. I fell in love.

Well, no. Not really love. "Soul-crushing teenage obsession" defines it more accurately. I was an awkward kid. Girls terrified me to the point that when I attempted to talk to them, my tongue would go into violent spasms. Ginette was an American exchange student, living in Greece for the summer. At some point in my trip, I summoned the courage to ask her to have dinner with me.

Other than the moment when I sneezed partially chewed bread all over my hand, the date went pretty well.

Alas, here I am, 20-plus years later, obliged to deliver the news that we did not fall madly in love and live happily ever after. I went back to Maryland. Ginette went back to New York. I sent her a letter to say hi. She sent me a letter to say hi. I never responded to her second letter. The end.

Okay, so my soul-crushing teenage obsession was short-lived, but during the three or four weeks I was stranded on the same Greek island as this girl, I got pretty wigged out. I was in love, damn it – that teenage kind of love that "nobody else can understand!" – especially my friend Anthony, who found my whole lovesick act highly annoying. Anthony was my friend in whom I usually confided *everything*, but he didn't want to hear about Ginette, so I poured my feelings into my journal. It felt therapeutic.

I had forgotten about Ginette completely until a few years ago when I was putting together a travel journaling class. I started plowing through some journals I hadn't read in years. Suddenly, there she was, smiling up at me from the page through my messy handwriting. Suddenly, there I was, sneezing bread all over myself.* An angst-ridden story from my youth suddenly seemed hilarious.

*I didn't actually journal about the bread incident at the time, but reading about the rest of the date was enough to dredge up that memory.

My perspective had changed ever so slightly. Somewhere over the years, I had learned two important life lessons: (1) girls aren't *that* scary, and (2) always swallow before sneezing.

I could have left it at that, but instead, I sat down and wrote about the experience after all these years. As much as I joke now about my teenage social awkwardness, the angst I felt at the time was torturous.* Journaling about it from an adult perspective, from a more experienced, more confident perspective, helped me realize how much I had grown emotionally. In my adolescence, I knew I was socially awkward... and I resigned myself to the thought that I would always be socially awkward. Analyzing the experience two decades later helped me understand we are not powerless over our personalities. If there are things about ourselves we don't like, we can change them. Often, we make these changes so gradually, we don't see how dramatic they ultimately are. My original journal from Greece showed me how far I'd come.

*Personal note to any awkward teens who are reading this book: The dorks who tell you your teenage years are "the best years of your life" are delusional. Life gets better!

I've re-journaled other trips as well, particularly my shoestring budget European blitz at age 20. Luckily on that trip, I poured a lot of emotion into my journals, so I have a lot to work with now. Going back and psychoanalyzing the 20-year-old me, years later, reminds me where I've come from. Seeing how much I've changed, it gives me optimism about the things I'm still figuring out.

Flight Simulator

Re-Journaling

Find an old travel journal entry. (If you don't have old travel journals, any past writing you have done will work. It can be a regular at-home journal, a letter, or an e-mail you have sent, for example.) Take a few minutes to reread what you wrote. Then, journal about it in the present context.

Here are some questions to help you get started:

- How does it feel now to read what you wrote then? What emotions are you feeling? How does your body feel as you recall the events?
- Can you remember how you were feeling at the time you wrote the original journal entry? Are you feeling differently as you read it now? Why or why not?
- How have you changed since you wrote the original journal entry?
- In what ways are you the same now as you were then?

Dave's Diaries

Vietnam and Hong Kong (Pre-Journaling)

As this book goes to press, my girlfriend Kattina and I are about to hop a flight to places that, for us, are uncharted territory. We're off to Hong Kong and Vietnam (after I make a brief stop in Dayton, Ohio).

My travel skills serve me well in Europe. They work okay elsewhere, but this upcoming trip is reminding me I only feel travel-savvy in certain parts of the world. When I travel to places that are totally foreign (Vietnam and Hong Kong, not Dayton) I must admit, I get jittery. Adding to my jitters is everything that's been going on at home.

Last winter, I spent three months on crutches after whacking my foot into a box of cassette tapes I should have thrown away in the 1980s. I was then diagnosed with a nerve disorder that makes walking ouchy. This medical drama forced me to push back two big book deadlines, crunching a mammoth amount of work into my spring.

So as you will now read, as I prepare for this desperately needed vacation, someone really should be coming for me with a straitjacket. If they can't catch me, I'll be winging my way across the Pacific Ocean on the day this book goes to the printer.

I'm determined to have a fun vacation once we land...but the following raw, unedited pre-journal entries capture my highly attractive panic and neurosis leading up to the trip. Will I survive the looming chaos? If I do, you'll find my Asian diaries at **traveljournaling.com.**

Five Weeks Before Departure: Needles and Dread

Walking down the street in Seattle a little while ago, I realized why I've been procrastinating all of my upcoming trip preparations. I've been procrastinating because there's one measly thing I have to do before I go that I don't want to do: I have to get vaccinations.

I need Hepatitis A and B – five shots in all. Those aren't

bad, but I also need Tetanus, and I still feel traumatized from too many Tetanus shots as a child.

I shouldn't be so whiny about my shots. I should feel lucky. The Typhoid vaccine you can now take orally, and the Hep shots are way nicer than the evil gamma globulin injections they used to jab into your hip with drain-pipe-sized needles.

Okay, so I'm a baby when it comes to shots, but this phobia of mine has stalled all the other things I should be doing to get ready – the most important of which is figuring out what to do once I'm on the ground. What a weird mental block! I think I've been procrastinating everything because of a couple of needles.

I'm feeling humbled by this trip. It's the first time in years I've felt nervous about going somewhere. Europe is easy for me now. Even Russia, two summers ago, felt tamer than it once did. The Middle East stresses me, but I know how to handle myself there. And my work in the South Pacific a few years ago hit me with some unanticipated culture shock, but it was relatively tame.

East Asia is a whole new part of the planet for me. Preparing to go there is reminding me what Europe feels like for first-time foreign travelers on my tours. I'm remembering now how intimidating foreign countries can sometimes feel.

In Europe, I'm a language nerd and a language snob. I can always understand enough of what's going on to find my way around. In Hong Kong and Vietnam, I've got no base. Yeah, I know how to manage with sign language and bad stick-figure drawings, but I won't have the same sense of getting what's happening around me.

I'm feeling more vulnerable to scams that target travelers than I feel when I'm in Europe. Asia will have more distractions. And yes, I'm well over my Turkish salad attack from when I taught in Ankara, but I still fear gastrointestinal nastiness – perhaps a bit more than the average traveler fears it.

I'm nervous about walking. My foot is still healing from my injury last fall. Vietnam will be my final test before tour season. I have to be well enough by May to lead groups around Europe all summer. If I can't get around Vietnam comfortably, I'll need to think about scaling back on my summer work.

And I'm embarrassed to admit I am nervous about traveling alone. Kattina will be with me the first eight days, but once she flies home, I'm on my own for four more. I used to love traveling solo. I still do when I know where I'm going. But this is all untrodden turf for me. It's been a long time since I've strayed so far from familiarity. Heh...my hyped-up nervousness is probably a sign that such a trip is long overdue.

Two Weeks Before Departure: Time Bandits

Eek! What the hell happened? I just looked at the calendar and thought, "Whoa! I'm leaving in only three weeks!" Then I looked again. It's not three weeks. It's two! I feel so not ready.

It's crazy enough that this will be some of my thickest culture shock ever. On top of that, I've hardly done a thing to prepare – hardly any research, not a single hotel booked, and I still don't know which country I'll spend my final four days in. Mainland China's been added to the list of possibilities, but they're in the throes of a political crisis at the moment – a situation that makes me ponder the ethics of traveling there.

These past six months have been a treadmill of stress. My foot injury threw my entire winter work schedule into chaos. I've had no time to sort out vacation logistics. But, hey, it's time to start sorting them out. Or not. I suppose when I land in Hong Kong, I'll exist there – planning or no planning. Considering we arrive late at night in both Hong Kong and Ho Chi Minh City though, I really should at least book hotels.

I survived my Tetanus shot last week, though not without severe whining. Isn't it funny that when I wrote my last pre-journal, I was assuming once I got over the vaccination hurdle, I'd start planning everything else?

My passport is at the Vietnamese embassy in Washington, DC. I had to mail it there for my visa. I hope they return it soon because if I do want to go to China, I need to mail it out again and get it back before I leave in 15 days.

As I sit here writing this, I'm noticing my heart has started racing. I feel like I should drop everything and figure out my plans – but work deadlines won't let me do that.

One Day Before Departure: Curse of the Black Goo

It's 3 a.m. here in Seattle, and I can't sleep. Perhaps that's a good thing because it's 6 a.m. in Ohio, and in Asia, it's almost dinner time. My sleep schedule is about to get so contorted anyway, I might as well get a jump on things.

I'm not sure what I was thinking when I decided to travel three time zones eastward for a writers' conference before turning around and going halfway around the world in the other direction to Asia. I have so much to get done in the next 24 hours, it's comical.

I won't whimper about my looming book deadline. That would be rude. I also have a conference proposal to write, an e-mail newsletter to send, tax forms to fill out, one last Hepatitis shot to endure, a bathroom to clean, and a bag to pack. Packing is something I should be good at by now, but how does one pack for both a writers' conference and a kayak trip through the Mekong Delta, and keep it all in one carry-on-sized bag?

Two days ago, I realized there was no way I was going to get everything done on time. I called the airline and postponed my flight to the conference in Ohio by a day. I went to bed feeling relieved, and I awoke yesterday morning to a peaceful sound – the sound of a babbling brook. I lay there in a half-slumber thinking, "How nice. A babbling brook is flowing through my bedroom." Then I opened my eyes.

Oh.

Oh no.

It was no babbling brook. It was my bathroom sink. Water and black goo were spewing up from the drain, onto the floor. I called my upstairs neighbors and asked them to stop showering. I called a plumber and asked him to rescue me. I called Kattina simply to whine. The flood stole several hours from my day, and I still have clean-up to do.

"Why now?" I lamented, but then I realized how lucky I was. Had it happened next week, showers from three other condo units would have drained into my bedroom – every day for two weeks until I came home.

And then there's my foot. Should I even get into that? Oh, why not? I'm already on a whiny rant.

Something not good has happened to my previously injured foot. I tweaked it somehow over the weekend. The swelling is back. I'm limping again – and just three days ago, Kattina looked at me and said, "Hey, you're not limping anymore!"

But it's got a few days to heal in Dayton before I begin traipsing around Hong Kong. The Erma Bombeck Writers' Workshop lasts through the weekend. Then I get 24 luxurious hours in economy class – Dayton to Chicago to San Francisco to Hong Kong – then two nights in Hong Kong before heading south to Vietnam.

I finally got hotels booked for my first couple of nights – and I've set up a biking/kayaking excursion and homestay in the Mekong Delta. I've quit trying to plan for the second half of the trip. I'm just going to wing it. I've got no more time to worry about travel preparations. Tomorrow, I'm out of here!

Postscript

Wow, this is strange – a story in my book, and I honestly don't know how it continues.

But by the time this book is published, my tales from the above journey will be posted on my website. I just might have to go check them out and find out what happened to me.

It's time for me to bundle up my manuscript, send it off to the printer, and jump on an airplane. But hey, part of the magic of writing a book is I don't have to write it in the order it gets read. I've already written the two final chapters. (You didn't think I'd leave you dangling, did you?)

So come on! Let's go answer the question everybody asks you when you come home.

CHAPTER 9

"How Was Your Trip?"

Sharing Your Journals with Others

Earlier, I encouraged you to "write like nobody's looking," to not censor your thoughts, dive deep into your mind and let the cultures around you draw out hidden parts of who you are. But what if somebody *is* looking? What if you *want* them to look?

It's time now to cast our words into the world for others to read. Don't worry. You get to decide how much you expose yourself, and to whom you expose yourself. Nobody gets to see your naked words without your permission.

There's a wide spectrum of ways you can take your words public – from a journal you pass around to a few select people, to blogging, to published essays in newspapers or magazines, or even your own book. Sharing your journals with other people – friends and family, or an audience of strangers – is different from private travel journaling. When you write for others, you might not include as many personal insights and experiences as you do in a private journal. Writing for an audience, it's okay to edit and censor, to decide what to share and what not to share.

The raw, personal journals you've written for yourself will serve as launching pads.

Journaling for People You Know

What's the first sentence out of everyone's mouth when you come home from a vacation?

"How was your trip?"

For most of us, travel means a break from our everyday routines. While we're out exploring, most of the world is doing what most of the world is usually doing: staying home. Most of us are lucky to get a couple of weeks to travel in any given year. So what do travel addicts do the rest of the year? Many of us travel vicariously, through the stories of others.

Sharing anecdotes from your journeys offers people a momentary escape of their own. Through the stories you bring home, they can imagine the places you've been. If you feed people enough details, they can picture themselves there. They hear the sounds and smell the smells. They get a sense of the emotions you've felt. They become just two degrees of separation from the characters whose paths you've crossed.

When we know others will read our journals, however, it affects our writing. You might have emotions too personal to share. Away from the people who know you best, you might have found yourself doing things outside of the normal "rules" we talked about in Chapter 6, and you might not feel comfortable revealing those behavioral detours. Then there's the simple issue of quality. Although you might return home with a collection of scrawl that triggers memories for yourself, you might not feel like your writing is polished enough to share with others. All of these factors leave you with two options when others will be reading your journals: Share the raw, unedited pages you've scribbled, as they are, or do some editing, censoring, and revising.

I recommend writing your "first draft" journals for yourself alone. You'll learn more from them that way. Write freely, and promise yourself you won't ever *have* to share anything with anyone you don't want to. If you travel intending from the start to share your journals with others, you're likely to hold back certain details. In doing so, you'll miss out on much of the powerful introspection that comes with journaling only for yourself. When I travel, I keep a private journal for myself, and edit it later for other readers. This takes extra time, but for me, it's worth it for the self-discovery aspect of the journey.

If you're like most people and don't have a lot of time for rewriting, consider this: Just as you can journal quickly while traveling, you can take a similar approach at home. If you've spent 10 to 20 minutes writing each day on your trip, an equal amount of time once your trip is finished should be plenty for a basic revision of each entry. You can, of course, put a lot more time into your public journals if you want to. If you want to create well-polished writing, you'll have to. It all depends on your own writing goals.

That having been said, some people prefer to share their journals without taking time to revise, and that's fine. There's just one important decision to make before you leave on your trip. Decide *before you go* whether you will share your "first draft" or whether you will keep it private and edit it later for others to read. If you go, uncertain as to whether or not you'll share your journal in its original form, you're bound to censor yourself..."just in case."

To Share or Not to Share? "How Much?" Is the Question

How do you decide what to include and what not to include in your public journals? Here are a few questions to ponder:

What am I comfortable sharing and what do I want to keep to myself? Writers face this dilemma in all sorts of genres. It's not just a journaling issue. On one hand, the more open you are, the more compelling your writing will be. On the other hand, putting words into print is like opening Pandora's box. Once someone has read something, you can't make them unread it. Ironically, many writers find it easier to share highly personal information with a large audience of strangers than with a small audience of loved ones. I faced this dilemma myself when I published my first book. There were things I had done in my travels I had no problem telling strangers about, but my mother was going to read the book too. In the end, I went with the attitude that the more I revealed, the better my book would be.* If I had been compiling the same collection of stories *only* for my family, however, I wouldn't have been so forthcoming. When you're getting started, I recommend erring on the cautious side, and seeing how comfortable you are having people read your work. After a while, you can test the waters more and take your readers deeper.

*And thanks, Mom! You took it well!

What do other people want to read? If you've been speed journaling, chances are you've written yourself into a few tangents that just sort of fizzle. Or you might have encountered something that was interesting to you, but that might not be so enthralling to others. If other readers aren't likely to be so fascinated by that topic, leave it out or condense it. First drafts almost always have extraneous details. When you edit your public journals, do some pruning. Weed out segments that aren't so compelling, and give your readers your most interesting stuff.

In what format do I want to present my journal? This depends on your goals or target audience. If you're writing for just a few people, you can photocopy your journals or send them out via e-mail. Putting your work into a blog or other website reaches larger audiences, as does publishing essays or articles in newspapers, magazines, or books. If you're ambitious, you could even publish a book of your own. These days, you don't necessarily need a large audience to do that. New self-publishing technologies are making it cheaper than it used to be to print up a few copies of a professional-looking book with a full-color glossy cover.

Do-It-Yourself Printing

You can go simple or you can go high-tech. If you're on a budget and just want a few copies of your journal to share, print it yourself and staple the pages together. Or, to get a little fancier for a relatively low price, have it bound at a copy shop. For a few dollars per copy, they can print and spiral-bind your journal in a plastic or cardboard cover.

If you want to get more elaborate, divide your journal into sections, based on the techniques we covered in Chapter 3. Include one section with a chronological account, another with themes you encountered along the way, another for the "cast of characters" you met in your wanderings, etc. Or, if you're assembling your public journal on a computer and have some basic layout skills, make your chronological journal the main focus, and add sidebars every few pages with themes, people, and verbal snapshots. Give each sidebar a category and a subtitle, such as "Verbal Snapshot: Platform 17 at the Mumbai Train Station," or "Cast of Characters: Zeke the Waiter."

If you've taken a visually artistic approach to your private journal, you can include those elements in a public journal too. With sketches, watercolors, etc., the high-tech way is to scan them and wrap your text around them. If you're not so computer savvy, photocopy your art from your original journal, paste it in your public journal, and fill the rest of the page with your words.

Such projects can take a little time, but assembling a journal like this is a fun way to reflect on your trip after it's finished. Your final product makes for a fun holiday gift, or a gesture of thanks for someone who has watched your home, watered your plants, fed your pets, or toilet papered your neighbor's trees for you in your absence.

Electronic Journaling: E-mail and Travel Blogging

Readers under 25 will laugh at me, but on my 1989 backpacking trip in Europe, I had three stops along the way where people could send me letters. Letters! Back in the 1980s, the Internet was not in widespread use by the general public.*

*And I had to walk to Europe! Barefoot! Through three feet of snow!

I gave people *poste restante* addresses in a couple of cities, where I could go to the post office and plow through a pile of letters to lots of people, hoping to find one or two for me. Then one day, I discovered e-mail. Keeping in touch with home changed forever.

E-mail is a great way to share stories from a journey in progress. To save time while traveling, set up a distribution list before you go, so each journal entry you send out goes to everyone on your list in a single mouse click. Internet cafés are everywhere these days – from modern cities to remote villages. In most parts of the world, you'll find a spot where you can get online for the local equivalent of a few dollars an hour.

If you want to write for a large audience, and you want to do so as you travel, blogging is the way to go. A basic blog is easy to set up, and many websites, such as **blogspot.com**, **livejournal.com**, and **myspace.com**, let you set up your blog for free. I host my blog at **typepad.com**. Typepad charges a small monthly fee, but after comparing them to several of the free services, I chose them for their advanced layout options and customer service. Other sites are devoted specifically to travel bloggers. You'll find links to some of these sites, as well as a link to my own blogs, at **traveljournaling.com**. A quick Internet search for "travel blogs" will also lead you to sites dedicated specifically to blogging about travel.

If you plan to blog from the road, set up your blog before leaving on your trip. Most people with basic Internet skills can get a simple blog going in an hour or two, but that's time you likely won't have while traveling.

The big disadvantage to online journaling, whether it's e-mail or blogging, is you're tied down to technology. Unless you're traveling with your own laptop, you can only type your journals when you find Internet access.

In my early days of travel blogging, lack of time frustrated me. When paying by the hour, the *tick-tock, tick-tock* sound inside my head distracted me from writing. Some Internet cafés were noisy, making it hard to concentrate. And if I was halfway through a blog entry when I needed to go, I could save the unfinished portion and get back to it later, but the same mood wasn't always with me at my next stop. I came up with an old-school solution to this problem: I now blog on paper before uploading.

Over the years, the books I journal in have gotten smaller and smaller. These days, I carry a pocket-sized spiral notebook. I often fill up several of them during a trip. I use these notepads for both my personal diaries and my blogs. If I'm suddenly struck by a blog idea, I'll scribble it down. Sometimes, I just jot a word or two on a list of topics I keep, so I remember the idea later. Or, if time allows, I write the entire blog entry in my notebook. Then, when I get to a computer, I can enter everything quickly without having to summon the inspiration that gripped me earlier.

Most blogs take on a different format from traditional journals. Each entry tells an individual story rather than, say, covering a full day's events. My own blog, whether I'm traveling or not, has a humorous focus. Here's a synopsis of travel-humor topics I blogged about while working in Greece for a month:

Gyromania: A pre-departure blurb about my obsession with *gyros* (pronounced "YEE-ros") – a tasty sandwich made from meat that's cooked on a spit and wrapped in pita bread – and my mission to consume 32 of these Greek fast food treats (they're small) during my 32 days in Greece.

Impostor Pelicans: About Peter the Pelican, the unofficial mascot on the island of Mykonos. I thought Peter was unique, but one day, I stumbled onto a gang of four pelicans, all of whom appeared to be arguing about who would play the role of Peter that day.

Jimmy the Gyros King: Meeting the man who has been running a gyros shop in the Greek islands for over 30 years.

Technology Bites: Palmtop computer and mobile phone malfunctions I've had while traveling.

Giorgos the Worm: I spotted a worm crawling around my hotel room, named him Giorgos, and adopted him as my mascot for a few hours.

Be Careful What You Bargain For: A tour member in the group I was working with returned to our bus one day, proud she had negotiated two guidebooks for the price of one. Several hours later, she realized the shop owner had sold her the Greek language version.

Protection for Your Funny Bone: Greek law requires motorcyclists to wear helmets while riding, but the law does not specify where on the body the helmets must be worn. As a result, some Greeks ride with helmets dangling around their elbows.

The Meltdown Continues: Technology continues to taunt me on my trip, and a blackout plunges the village of Gythio into darkness.

The Balcophone: A new low-tech communication technique the other tour guide and I devised to get each other's attention.

Prehistoric Porn: The National Museum in Athens had amusing English translations on its erotic statues – and rules to thwart tourists from being disrespectful.

The Cat Who Ate Nafplio: Most of Greece's stray cats are scrawny. I speculate on how one particularly large feline got so chubby.

Homeward Bound: My flight home...and the fact that I

only managed to gobble down 22 gyros, though I did break my previous year's record of 17.

In a one-month journey, I ended up with 12 fun mini-essays (with an ongoing "gyrometer" updating my daily gyros progress). As a humor writer, I went with an odd mix of topics, some of which were rather mundane (such as a worm in my hotel room) but to which I could attach a quick, amusing anecdote.

You might take a different approach. You might stick to a specific theme, like sights or interesting people, or a consistent tone, such as self-discovery. Or you might choose a random topic each time you blog. That's one great thing about the spirit of blogging; blogs have evolved without the pressure to sound organized or professional with everything you write.

Keep in mind, particularly if you want to build an audience, that people are not interested in every little detail. Online attention spans are short. People want highlights in short, capsulized blurbs that fill no more than a couple of computer screens. Some blog entries are as short as two or three sentences.

One final note about blogging and chronology: Most blogging software is set up with a default so that each entry shows the time you uploaded it. You can usually adjust that timestamp. I sometimes find I have scribbled two or three quick entries in my notebook over the course of a few days, but I upload them all at the same time. When I upload, I adjust the timestamp to reflect the time I wrote each entry, not the time I uploaded it.

Writing for Print Publications

The more serious you get about travel journaling, the more you will start to identify themes you can develop into well-honed essays. You can publish these essays in newspapers, magazines, or books. Not only that, you can get paid for your work.

If this is a goal for you, keep in mind that these days, few publications are interested in generic travel journals. Editors want essays on specific topics, unique stories that capture the spirit of a place and make readers feel like they are there. Don't just write about a place you've been. Go for a specific story.

On a trip to Finland, I wrote about sauna etiquette, and my confusion about whether or not to wear a swimsuit in a public sauna. In Ireland, I covered the impromptu folk music sessions that spring up in small-town pubs. In a small French hilltown, I wrote a humor essay about traveler's burnout, about watching a duck in a river quack very loudly, and how I envied the duck, wishing I too could quack loudly in public to vent my travel fatigue. Only once have I ever published an essay based solely on a destination, as opposed to something I experienced in that destination. That destination was a small town in Wales called Llanfairpwllgwyngyllgogerychwyrndrobwllllantysiliogogogoch. You can guess what the focus of the essay was.

Humor is a favorite approach for many travel essayists. Another is self-discovery – learning a lesson about life or ourselves by being in a foreign place. Many publications also purchase articles about unusual sites, attractions, or festivals. In this last case, they usually want more than just an essay, however. They want interviews with people who live there, and meticulously checked facts. It's critical when publishing professionally that if you quote specific people, you quote them accurately. Unlike private journals, where it's okay to write other people's words as well as you can recall them, if you quote someone in a public forum, you can be sued for inaccuracies.

Who buys these essays? For starters, many newspaper travel sections need articles. Newspaper pay is relatively low, but many papers will let you sell your article simultaneously to multiple, non-competing markets. My Irish folk music article appeared on St. Patrick's Day in both the *Portland Oregonian* and the *Dallas*

Morning News. Editors in both cities were fine with that because the chance of anyone reading both papers on the same day was slim. If you pitch an essay to multiple publications, let the editors know you're doing this. Different newspapers have different policies. Request a copy of their writers' guidelines, and tell the editors where else you are submitting your story.

Magazines are another good market for essays, but get familiar with a magazine before you submit something. Few things annoy editors more than writers who pitch stories that don't fit the magazine's tone or format. Sending a story about youth hostelling, for example, to a magazine that specializes in upscale travel is a waste of your time and the editor's.

Beginning travel freelancers often make the mistake of limiting their pitches to travel publications. Many travel magazines do not publish first-person essays at all, and several that used to have sadly gone out of business. Look for other themes within your travel stories. Remember that feta-and-rhinoceros omelet we munched on in Chapter 3? Pitch that story to a food magazine. A sauna article could fit nicely in a health and fitness magazine. My Irish music article might run in a music magazine, or even a publication about food and beverages since the sessions take place in pubs. Many airline in-flight magazines also publish travel essays.

Writer's Market lists several thousand publications that buy freelance work. The book is updated annually, with information such as the types of articles each magazine wants, how they want you to submit them, to whom you should submit them, their preferred word count, etc. For beginning freelancers, the book includes great tips on getting started, industry etiquette, and so on.

Writing for Books

Several companies publish occasional books of travel essays – usually on a particular theme. One nice thing about publishing in books is they have a longer shelf life than newspapers and magazines.

Travelers' Tales, one of the biggest and best established series of travel essay compilations, has an ongoing list on their website (**travelerstales.com**) of themes and destinations they want stories about. Most of their books focus on either a particular country or region, or a particular topic, such as women's travel, spiritual travel, international food, or humor. *Lonely Planet*, the well-known guidebook series, has also produced a few compilations of travel essays.

If you're especially ambitious, your journals might even evolve into a book of your own. It happened to me – though it took 17 years from the time I conceived my first travel book idea to the day the book was published. If you've never published professionally, be realistic in your goals. Publishers and agents will take you more seriously if you can show them a portfolio of clips you've published, so short articles are usually an easier starting place. But if you've had a particularly compelling journey, and you feel your writing is of professional quality, travel is a hot genre. (And if you don't feel you are able to produce pro-quality writing yet, but you want to, keep practicing! Join writers' groups, take classes, solicit feedback from others, and write like a maniac! Over time, your writing will improve.)

"But Dave," you say, "I really, really want to publish a book, and I want to do it *now*!"

Okay. You can.

Breaking into the mainstream book industry is getting harder and harder. Big publishing houses these days pour the bulk of their budgets into established writers who are guaranteed to sell. At the same time, however, self-publishing is becoming more popular, less stigmatized, and a lot less expensive than it once was.

New "Print-On-Demand" or "POD" technology enables publishers to zap out books one copy at a time, rather than printing several thousand in one fell swoop. Authors submit a manuscript and work with the publisher on a cover design. The book is stored in a computer, and when someone orders a copy, out it comes with a few mouse clicks. This technology makes it easy for anyone to publish a book. Want to impress your friends and family over the holidays? You'll have to invest some time and cash, but you can take either your basic travel journals, or a collection of essays that have evolved from them, and turn them into a book – paperback or hardback – that looks just like any other perfect-bound book you'd find in stores.

Spend some time researching POD publishers to find the company that's best for you. The big, easy-to-find publishers aren't always the best. Inkwater Press, the publisher of this book, has a POD division, and I can attest to the fact that they're nifty people to work with.* If you only plan to print a few copies, **Lulu.com** offers an exceptional value in that they don't charge any set-up fees. With Lulu, if you do your own layout, you'll pay less than ten dollars a book with no extra costs.

*Honestly! They're not paying me extra to tell you this! Although, hey, Jeremy, if you want to toss me a bonus for the plug, ummm....

Most POD publishers charge a set-up fee of a few hundred bucks. Once you've signed with them, you'll submit your manuscript via e-mail or on a disk, and then work with the publisher to design a cover. Many companies offer additional services such as proofreading, editing, and marketing assistance, but these extras can get pricey. If you choose to, you can list your book on bookseller websites such as Amazon and set your price. The publisher handles distribution, takes a portion of the profits from each copy sold, and sends you the rest.

Listing your book online does not guarantee sales. Don't expect to get rich unless you plan to spend lots of time promoting your work. But even if you don't make *The New York Times*

Bestseller List, POD publishing can be a fun way to print up a small batch of books to give away as gifts.

Connecting the World

Sharing your travel journals lets people experience a trip they couldn't go on themselves. It gives you the opportunity to introduce people to cultures they might not be familiar with. As contrived as this might sound, I really believe the more we all get to know people who think and live differently from us, the more potential we have in our world for peaceful coexistence.* Some of the ideas in this chapter might seem more involved than you have time for. If going out and publishing your travel tales, or putting them online for strangers to read, or spending time and money to bind them into a book, is more than you wish to tackle, keep it simple, and stick to the basics. And even if you write a personal journal solely for yourself, and never share your *written* words with others, rereading your journal from time to time will keep your stories bright in your own mind so you'll have great anecdotes to share in one-on-one conversations.

*See? I'm more than just a snarky weirdo!

Dave's Diaries

Helsinki, Finland

Confusing situations, frustrating as they can be in the moment, often make for great humor essays. The following story, about a sauna experience I had in Helsinki, originally appeared in my online travel journals. I later sold a version of the story to Lonely Planet, who published it in their collection of essays, *Rite of Passage: Tales of Backpacking 'Round Europe*.

Saunas: The Naked Truth

I was sweating profusely in the 88-degree heat. That's 88 Celsius – 190 Fahrenheit. But it wasn't the heat in the sauna that was making me uncomfortable. What was making me uncomfortable was sitting there alone, screamingly naked in a public place, not sure if I was supposed to *be* naked in this public place.

I'm not one of those prudish Americans who's terrified of being seen naked in public – as long as everyone else is going about their nakedness without paying me any attention. But sometimes in Europe, it's hard to know the rules.

It had been a dreary, drizzly day in Helsinki. My tour group had free time to explore the city. Rather than eating waffles in the rain at the outdoor market, I went back early to the ferry that would take us to Stockholm overnight. For less than 40 US dollars, I could have a one-hour massage and 90 minutes in the ship's spa.

A lot of people have the wrong idea about so-called "Swedish massages." They don't feel good while you're having one, and they're too intense to be done by petite Scandinavian cuties named Inga. But they are effective in beating your tension into submission.

For 55 minutes, a burly Finnish man induced more

pain on my back than I knew could be induced using only two thumbs. The first time I screamed, he muttered, "Yes, your muscles are very tight." The second time, he offered to lighten up, which he did for all of 30 seconds. But I breathed into the pain and let my muscles buckle under the pressure. I walked out feeling blissfully mellow – albeit a little bruised.

There were four other activities: soak in the whirlpool, sit in the steam room, take a sauna, or drink beer. Never mind that beer is not usually recommended while participating in other dehydrating activities. This was Finland, and drinking beer is how Finns replace their fluids after a night with a vodka bottle.

The whirlpool had room for about 10 people – potentially strangers sitting close together, so swimsuits made sense here. The steam room right next to the whirlpool also looked like a keep-yourself-covered kind of a place. I checked with the attendant to be sure. She nodded. Then she handed me a key to the locker room and sauna. That's when my confusion began.

My other sauna experiences have always been uncovered. Scandinavians don't have the hang-ups about nudity that Americans do. On warm, sunny days, I've seen people strip completely naked in city parks. In public saunas, I've encountered separate rooms for men and women. But here, there was no sign on the door to indicate that. I was the only person in the room so far, with no way to know when someone else might walk in. I dreaded the thought of an innocent Finnish granny entering as I sat in an inappropriate state of undress, and having a heart attack at the sight of Dave, the Naked American Pervert.

The only scenario worse than that was being a clothed American in a place where one was not supposed to be clothed. I imagined the comments on the boat later that evening: "Hey Toivo, there goes the American who wore the swimsuit in the sauna! I wonder what he has to hide!"

I couldn't ask the attendant. I had already asked her about the steam room. She'd think I was obsessed. I wished someone else would come in – anyone – so I could observe and figure out the protocol. I couldn't get the image of the dead granny on the sauna floor out of my head. I decided to keep my suit on.

The purpose of a sauna is to sweat every drop of water out of your body, then shock yourself with a quick, cold shower. Repeat the process as many times as you can stand it until your blood screams through your veins at the speed of light. The sauna's interior is all wood. In the corner is a heater with rocks on top. Scoop water out of a nearby bucket onto the rocks and a wall of steam hits you like dragon's breath.

After 10 minutes of sweating, I decided a swimsuit in a 190 degree room was ridiculous. I showered and went in for round two with only a towel around me.

The towel covered me down to the middle of my calves. It was far too warm. No, this was definitely a place where one was to be naked. I untucked the towel from around my waist and assumed a discreet posture.

I sat. I sweated. I worried. I couldn't stop thinking about the granny.

I finally decided I needed to leave. The sauna was too stressful. I knew the rules elsewhere in the spa.

From the whirlpool, I watched the locker room door but no one went in. After 20 minutes of bubbles, I was bored. I headed for the Turkish bath, which was delightful – steamy and herb-scented. I relaxed and sighed and looked up at the ceiling. That's when I spotted the steam valves. They creeped me out. They made me think of Nazi gas chambers. I got up and left.

I wanted to go back into the sauna, but I was determined not to until I knew the rules. There was only one activity left while I waited. Beer.

I sat at the bar and sipped slowly, never taking my eyes off the locker room door. Finally, just as I was about to give up and leave, success! A married couple walked in. They paid at the counter, rented swimsuits, and were sent to change – in separate rooms. So there *were* separate saunas. And if they were separating a married couple, it was certainly so naked strangers of the opposite sex would not be squished together in close quarters. I had the rules figured out now – I thought.

I swigged my last gulp of beer and strolled confidently for the locker room. There was the man who had just paid. It was the only time in my life I have been happy to see a hairy, flabby, naked man. He nodded. I nodded. He headed for the shower. I undressed and headed for the sauna.

I opened the door a crack and peeked inside. I slammed the door in horror. There were two men inside. And they were wearing swimming suits!

I didn't get it. If we were supposed to wear swimsuits, why did they bother with separate rooms for men and women? And why was Hairy Flabby Naked Man showering right outside without anything on? I went back to my locker and re-suited.

As I entered, one of the men inside moved over to make room for me. I thanked him in Norwegian. He answered in Swedish, but his accent was something else. He was as foreign as I was. What did he know?

I sighed. Hairy Flabby Naked Man was about to walk, fully exposed, into a room full of foreigners. He was going to feel awkward dangling before us. But with three of us and one of him, I wondered if he'd feel intimidated enough to cover himself.

When he entered wearing a black Speedo, I gave up. All I knew for sure was that Hairy Flabby Naked Man looked far more offensive in a skimpy black Speedo than he did *au naturel.*

I sweated and showered a couple of times. One by one, my sauna mates left until I was alone again. Then, out in the showers, I could hear a group of about six rowdy, drunken Finns. I was too sober to be around rowdy drunken Finns, clothed or not. And my 90 minutes were just about up. I went up to my cabin, undressed one last time, and showered in blissful privacy.

CHAPTER 10

Empty Notebook Syndrome

Finding Time and Motivation

Looking at my bookcases, I see seven books about writing, three books about reducing clutter, four about overcoming stress and anxiety, six on interpersonal communication, two about yoga and meditation, two about investing, three about procrastination,* and too many books to count on languages I don't have time to learn.

*how to overcome it, not how to do it

I've read a couple of these books from cover to cover, skimmed through others, and allowed most of them to gather dust on my shelf in the hope that some night, a magical book gnome will enter my home and whisper the wisdom from these books in my ear while I am sleeping. Then, when I wake up the next morning, I will be transformed by the mighty new knowledge I attained subliminally during the night.

Say to yourself, llamas like me...

This has yet to happen.

A large percentage of the books people buy never get read. If you've read this far, congratulations. If you're like me, however, you've read self-improvement or how-to books before, and not managed to do much with whatever they've taught you. Now that you've read this book, flown in the flight simulator, learned all of these nifty writing techniques, and endured all of my stupid jokes, you deserve to create some extraordinary travel journals on your next big trip. All too often when we read books like this, we get great new ideas, but we don't find the time or motivation to implement them. I am determined to not let that happen to you.

If you've read this far, I want you to be a travel journaling superhero. I want you to be so prolific in your future journaling endeavors that one day, your efforts will inspire a Super Travel Journaler action figure and brand of chewable vitamins. So in this final chapter, we're going to confront one of the biggest curses against prospective journalers: Empty Notebook Syndrome.

Before we part ways, and you go off on your own in the journaling world, let's take an honest look at the realities of time and motivation – and learn how to work with those realities, rather than fighting them, so your chances of returning home with an empty journal are significantly diminished.

Pen-to-Page Resuscitation

"Even the most dedicated traveler journalers are travelers first and journalers second."

Those words were first written in sixth century B.C. China by a wise philosopher named...oh wait. No, I'm thinking of a different quote. Let's start again.

"Even the most dedicated traveler journalers are travelers first and journalers second."

Those words were first written in Chapter 2 by a kind of dorky writer guy. He would like to remind you of that quote right now.*

*He is also wondering why he has suddenly started referring to himself in the third person.

Your time to write while traveling is limited. Remember

that, and you've conquered one of the most inhibiting misconceptions to plague many journalers. You might have an occasional day when you find a couple of free hours to go on a writing binge, but on most days, if you're journaling for more than 10 or 20 minutes, you are probably missing other experiences.

If you find yourself gasping for literary breath as you struggle to catch up with events from several days ago, you run the risk of falling so far behind that you never recover. Your journal at this point is in critical condition. You need to resuscitate it.

If you're more than three days behind in your writing, it's time for some emergency journal triage. Cut corners on the missing days and get back to writing about the present as quickly as possible. There are a couple of ways to do this. Either try the five-sentence-a-day technique described in Chapter 3, or allow yourself three minutes of time for each day you've fallen behind to jot down a few quick sentences, or even just a list of words – events and impressions that will trigger memories later. The point is: catch up fast and get back on track. You can always go back and fill in the blanks later. You might even scribble the words, "Emergency Journal Triage" at the top of your catch-up entries to distinguish them from your other journaling.

Flight Simulator

Emergency Journal Triage

Let's practice this right now. Grab your notebook and do the following:

Think for a moment about what you did four days ago. In three minutes or less, describe your day in a *maximum* of five sentences. Then, do the same for three days ago, two days ago, and yesterday. Finish off with whatever has happened so far today.

How much time did you need to remember what you did four days ago? Comparatively, how much time did you need to recall what you've done today?

Journaling about whatever happened several days ago doesn't only slow us down because we have a lot of days to recap. It's also cumbersome because it takes more time and brain energy to recall those older details. That's why catching up quickly is important. Splash down what you remember from previous days, and get back to writing about today while today is still fresh.

Of course, it's better not to have to fall back on this technique. It's best to keep your journals up-to-date as you go, but this isn't always possible. We face a couple of different challenges in keeping our journals on track.

- Finding the time to write
- Finding the motivation to write

Let's examine each of these challenges and look at ways to overcome them.

Finding Time

Knowing how to write a great travel journal is useless if you can't find time to write. Finding that time can be tough though. Every journey has short slices of downtime. Learn to notice and write in those moments, and you'll get your journaling done without sacrificing other experiences.

How often in any given trip do we wait? We wait for planes, trains, or buses. We wait for a meal to arrive at our table. We wait for our travel partner to wake up or shower. We wait in lines. We wait for performances or events to begin. We wait for our feet to stop aching. We wait for a restaurant or shop to open. We wait for an Internet terminal to become available. We wait to arrive at our next destination.

That's a lot of waiting.

When I catch a train in Europe, I get to the station at least 20 minutes early. I allow a few extra minutes to find the right track – but usually, I can find that track in two or three minutes. That's 17 minutes when I'm standing around, waiting, staring at the track as if my train might magically appear sooner if I stare hard enough. It's a perfect length of time for some speed journaling.

Is it the ideal writing environment? Nope. Sure, I get distracted by announcements, people around me, or other trains pulling into or out of the station. But if we wait for the ideal writing environment to reveal itself, that time might never come. Writing in a crowded, noisy environment is hard for some people, but with practice, you'll get better at tuning out distractions. And you might not do your best writing in such environments, but mediocre writing is better than no writing.

Time in transit is another time to catch up. Sometimes on trains, I want to kick back and enjoy the scenery, but scenery can grow redundant. I use a few minutes of my ride to write. I journal on planes and buses too. Messy handwriting on bumpy roads? No problem. Potholes just add artistic squiggles to the page. They're part of the experience.

Traveling companions can distract you from journaling time. They want to go play and they want you to come. But hopefully, your partner is bathing on a regular basis. When he or she heads for the shower, let that be your cue to write. Let them know you'll be doing this, and ask them to remind you to journal before they hit the shower.

Another time I get a lot of journaling done is when I do laundry. When I'm on the road for weeks on end, I wash my clothes in my hotel sink a lot, but every couple of weeks, I also hit a laundromat. In big, foreign cities, I'm not going to leave my clothes alone while they wash, for fear they might wander off. So I bring my journal with me. Usually, I find a big chunk of time to write.

I say "usually" because sometimes I meet fascinating people in laundromats. Perplexed by the washing machine instructions in Paris one time, I asked an elderly lady who lived in the neighborhood to help me. We ended up having a long conversation about how US-French relations had changed over the decades. In that moment, I wasn't going to tell her I couldn't talk because I needed to write. But on other occasions, I've been faced with a choice between writing and staring at soap suds for an hour.*

*And, for the record, Parisian soap suds are no more elegant than your soap suds at home.

Many other "waiting times" are times when you won't want to write. If you pause to rest your feet at a café, you might want to spend that time people-watching or striking up a conversation with someone at a nearby table. In a fancy restaurant, it might not be appropriate to pull out your notebook. But if you keep your journal with you during the day, you'll be surprised how many moments of downtime you do find. Even if you don't have time for a complete entry, jotting down a few thoughts for a couple of minutes means you'll have more memory triggers later.

Flight Simulator

Finding Time

For the next few days, carry a notebook with you wherever you go. Look for moments when you have a few free minutes to write. In those moments, write whatever you

> like. You can journal about your day. You can journal about a past or present trip. Just write something, and see how much you get written in these slices of time.

When you do the above exercise, you won't always finish what you start, but once you get used to writing in quick bursts, you might be surprised how much you do write throughout your day. Again, remember, your goal here should not be perfection. Your goal should be writing something – period.

Finding Motivation

I have a confession. As I sit here trying to motivate you, I am the King of Procrastination in some areas of life. I take up jogging at least twice a year. I run for a few days. Then I forget, or I get sick, or too swamped with work, or too annoyed with Seattle's winter drizzle to keep going.

I have friends who run marathons. Running is their life. They talk about the "runner's high" they get after the first few miles. I'd like to experience that runner's high, but I conk out and lose my routine. I keep thinking if I could just maintain a consistent schedule, I might grow to love running.

Getting started is often the hardest part with a new endeavor. Once we get into the habit of doing something, and make it part of our daily routine, it comes naturally. We can't imagine existing without doing it.

I've reached that momentum with travel journaling. I can't imagine not writing when I'm on a trip. When I don't journal, or blog, or find some way to capture my experiences in words, it's as if something is missing.

How can you reach the point with your own journaling where you *need* to write when you travel, where writing is as natural each day as brushing your teeth? The more you journal, the more second-nature it will become.

When you start a new routine, the first few weeks are most important. If you can stick to a schedule for the first three or four weeks, you build momentum that helps you keep going. Unfortunately, many of us are trapped in the evil American tradition of only two weeks of vacation per year. So start journaling before you begin traveling. Write for 10 minutes every day. It doesn't matter what you write. You can pre-journal about an upcoming journey, or post-journal about past travels, or simply write about your current day. But write. Schedule a consistent time and place. You can do it first thing in the morning, during your lunch break, in the late afternoon, or just before bed. You can do it at home, at work,* at your favorite local hangout – wherever you like. Just get in the habit of writing something, somewhere, sometime, every day.

*When the boss isn't looking, perhaps!

If you get this routine going before you depart, you're halfway there. There's just one problem: When you travel, you break most of your daily routines. Many of us travel to escape our daily routines. So before you leave, think about how you'll adapt your journaling routine to your new surroundings.

Some of the downtime moments I noted above come with built-in reminders. Your travel partner's showering time, for example, becomes your cue. Look for other cues in your surroundings. When I lived in Turkey, not being Muslim, I took the late morning call to prayer that bellowed through the city as my reminder to write. (Be careful with this one. I wrote in the privacy of my apartment. Depending on where you are, when it's time for prayers, if you are not praying yourself, you are expected to at least stop other activities for a few minutes out of respect.) There are things you will do in your travels on a consistent basis – eating, sleeping, going out for the first time each day, or brushing your teeth. Attach your journaling to another activity you already do consistently. Make it part of your daily dental regimen, and don't brush your teeth until you've written for at least 10 minutes. Are you the sort of person who can't survive without a mid-day coffee? Perfect! Go get your coffee and bring your journal with you. Or... tell yourself you can't have your coffee until you've journaled.*

*Depending on your level of caffeine addiction, this might make for some cranky journal entries, but it will motivate you!

Reward Yourself

If writing consistently is a struggle for you, then when you do manage to do it, you deserve a reward! Knowing you'll get such a reward becomes one more motivator. These rewards can be simple. Each day you write, allow yourself a cappuccino, an ice cream, dessert with dinner, anything you enjoy, but can also exist without on the days you don't accomplish your task. If you absolutely *must* have your afternoon coffee and you're going to go get it whether you journal or not, that should not be your reward. Make it something special, which you don't need, but which will make you happy.

CHOCOLATE

You can also go for bigger, long-term rewards. Choose a daily dollar amount (or an amount in the local currency). Choose whatever amount fits your own budget – one dollar a day, or 1,000 dollars a day. For the sake of explanation, let's go with 10. Let's say you're on a three-week trip, and you hope to write every day. Realistically speaking, let's say you miss a few days, but you generally keep up with your schedule. At the end of 21 days, you've written on 17 of them. At the end of your trip, reward yourself with 10 dollars per day for the days you did write, and you've earned yourself 170 dollars to buy a special souvenir, a swanky last night's dinner, splurgy accommodations, whatever appeals to you.

If you go with a monetary reward, it's important you stick to your agreement with yourself. Consider writing a contract at the front or back of your journal so you don't waver. Do not spend more money on your reward than the amount you have earned – but far more importantly, *do* follow through with your reward. Buyer's remorse is not allowed. Don't cheat yourself out of a promise you've made to yourself. If you start feeling like you really shouldn't spend the money after all, spend it anyway. In the long run, a little overspent cash is far less of a loss than the loss of a major source of motivation.

Get creative. Find a reward system that works for you. You could even start out with a double reward – dessert on each day you write, *and* a cumulative prize at the end.

I've used this system in lots of areas of my life – from writing, to cleaning my condo, to flossing. It's even helping me get this book written right now.*

*Hmmm...I really should try it with jogging.

Go!

Journeys are gifts we give ourselves. Even if you are very lucky, and have someone else footing the bill for your journey, *you* are still giving yourself a gift just by going. Too many people have opportunities to travel, but choose to stay home – fearful of the unknown, shackled by their everyday rut, tied down to commitments that don't have to tie them down if they would seek creative solutions. We can't always travel right away, but we *can* always be planning, scheming, chiseling away at the things that keep us home so that someday in the hopefully not-too-distant future, we can go explore places we dream of visiting.

Where do you dream of traveling to that you haven't been? *What are you doing to get there?*

All too often, people talk about places they want to go..."someday." Well, "someday" will only come if you start making steps toward it. Chinese philosopher Lao Tzu put it nicely when he wrote, "A journey of a thousand miles begins with a single step."*

Take a step today.

We live in a world of instant gratification.

*Yeah, that's the quote I was thinking of earlier.

That thirst for instant gratification can hold us back from getting what we want. If something isn't immediately within our reach, we label it unobtainable.

Can't afford to travel right now? Okay, what can you afford? A dollar a day? Put a dollar in a shoebox each day. In three years, you'll have nearly 1,100 dollars. That should cover a plane ticket to lots of places.

"But Dave, three years is so far away! Putting a dollar aside each day will take forever!"

Too bad you were thinking that way three years ago, huh?

Can't afford a dollar a day? Then start with a quarter.

What else might be stopping you from traveling? How can you create a long-term plan to work around those obstacles?

Can't get time off of work? Sounds like you need to talk to your boss. When *can* you get time?

Your spouse or significant other doesn't like to travel? I hear that sometimes from people in my tour groups. Some travel alone. Others convince their partner to come along – but that convincing can take time. He or she might not come around right away. You might need to have several chats. Have the first one tonight.

Health concerns getting in your way? Talk to your doctor and find out if they really are the obstacles you think they are. If they are, if you can't go as far as you would like to, where *can* you go? What *can* you do?

Your kids are too young to travel? I hear that a lot too. If my parents had thought that way, you probably wouldn't be reading this book right now. My younger brother, Steve, was four when we moved to England and visited France, Belgium, Holland, Switzerland, Greece, and Tunisia. He had a great time.*

*And sure, he's a little bit strange now, but I don't think that's Tunisia's fault.

Flight Simulator

Excuses, Excuses

Make a list of at least five places you want to travel to. Pick one of them. Next, make a list of all the reasons you can't go there right now. Then, for each reason, write one or both of the following:

- What you are going to do to eliminate that reason.
- A rebuttal to your reason.

If you start actively planning a trip, you can make it happen. Sometimes dreams take time and patience – and just like food tastes better when we're super hungry, finally arriving at the moment when we've turned a challenging dream into reality can feel blissful. It can also feel frightening, but fear can be good. That's how you're supposed to feel when you step out of your comfort zones.

As far as your journaling goes, keep at it. Reading this book will teach you the skills to become a great travel journaler, but reading alone will not make you great. Journaling will. The more you write, the better you'll get. There will be days on your trips when you can't wait to get something down on paper. There will be other days when journaling feels like a chore. Try anyway on those days to write *something.* I've discovered over the years that sometimes when I think my writing is bad, it's actually not. It's my mood that's bad. When I go back later to read what I wrote, my writing sounds just fine.

Then again, some days I do write utter drivel. Improvement rarely comes in a straight line. Sometimes, we backslide, but if we keep writing, our cumulative result is positive. If, on some days, you're convinced your writing really is bad, congratulate yourself – for writing your way through a challenging moment in your journaling life. Many people give up in those moments.

The difference between a good writer and a bad writer is not that a good writer always cranks out top-quality literature and a bad writer doesn't. The real difference is a good writer keeps going on bad days, and a bad writer gives up.

Hey, you know what? I've just finished writing a book! Wow! I'm going to go have a beer and take a nap now before I catch that flight to Vietnam. Before I do, however, please allow me to recap a few key points:

- When traveling, your writing time is limited. Cover the key points and then get on with your trip.
- Travel journals are usually first drafts. First drafts are not supposed to be perfect.
- Write like nobody's looking.
- Prioritize memory triggers, not flowery prose.
- Show, don't tell. Scan your five senses and be descriptive.
- There's no such thing as a wrong emotion. Be honest with yourself. Then ask yourself, "Really?" and "Why?"
- When you fall behind, cut corners and catch up quickly.
- Look for short moments of downtime in which you can write.
- Reward yourself when you write.
- Have fun!
- Eat chocolate!
- Break the rules!

I started journaling about my travels at age seven. Years later, my travel journals launched me on a pretty cool career path. My goal in these last ten chapters has been to teach you what I've learned along the way. If you have other techniques to share, exercises to suggest, victories to brag about, questions to pose, fan mail, hate mail, a burning desire to hire me for something, or a super-fabulous chocolate chip cookie recipe to bestow, please drop me an e-mail. You'll find my contact info at **traveljournaling.com**.

About Dave Fox

Dave Fox started traveling the world at age seven, and he's been journaling ever since. Based in Seattle, Washington, he has lived in England, Norway, and Turkey, and visited more than 40 countries.

His first book, *Getting Lost: Mishaps of an Accidental Nomad*, won the Erma Bombeck Writers' Workshop Book Proposal Contest in 2004. The second edition was published by Inkwater Press in 2008.

Dave works as a freelance writer, speaker, and international tour guide. His travel journaling classes have been recommended in the *Wall Street Journal*. He offers entertaining and informative presentations on a variety of topics for businesses and other organizations. He's a veteran tour guide for European travel guru Rick Steves, and also leads his own travel journaling tours.

To contact Dave, or for more information about his work, please visit his websites: TRAVELJOURNALING.COM and DAVETHEFOX.COM.